DAMBUSTER

A Life of
Guy Gibson, VC, DSO*, DFC*

by

SUSAN OTTAWAY

Pen & Sword
AVIATION

First published in Great Britain in 1994
Reprinted in 1996 and again in 2003
Published in this format in 2007 and reprinted in 2008 by
PEN & SWORD AVIATION
an imprint of
Pen & Sword Books Ltd
47 Church Street
Barnsley
South Yorkshire
S70 2AS

ISBN 978 1 84415 6 054

A CIP catalogue record for this book is
available from the British Library.

Printed and bound in Great Britain
by MPG Biddles Ltd, King's Lynn, Norfolk

Pen & Sword Books Ltd incorporates the Imprints of
Pen & Sword Aviation, Pen & Sword Maritime, Pen & Sword Military,
Wharncliffe Local History, Pen & Sword Select,
Pen & Sword Military Classics and Leo Cooper.

For a complete list of Pen & Sword titles please contact
PEN & SWORD BOOKS LIMITED
47 Church Street, Barnsley, South Yorkshire, S70 2AS, England
E-mail: enquiries@pen-and-sword.co.uk
Website: www.pen-and-sword.co.uk

DAMBUSTER

CONTENTS

ACKNOWLEDGEMENTS

My interest in Guy Gibson began when, as a teenager, I read his book *Enemy Coast Ahead*. Over the years I often tried to find out more about him, but discovered that, with the exception of the accounts of the Dams raid of 16–17 May, 1943, very little had been written. Accordingly, I decided that, if I were to ever discover anything more about the man who had captured my attention all those years ago, I would have to research the subject myself. This book is the result of that research.

I am indebted to the following people who provided me with information, photographs and personal memories and to those who helped me to sort out technical details: James Bamford, Ralph Barker, Wynne Barlow, Mr Bastable, Tony Bastiaanse, the late Sebastian Bastiaanse, Squadron Leader Oscar Bridgman (rtd), Mrs M. Brindley-Auger, Mr B. Briscoe, Robin Brooks, Ray Callow, Group Captain R. Churcher (rtd), Colin Cole, Barbara Cooke, Eddie Coward, Mr T. Cushing, Mr Dougan, David Farnon, Basil and Jean Feneron, Douglas Garton, Ruth Gibson, Elizabeth Gilliland, Harold Godfrey, Peter Green, Ray Griffiths, Stan Harpham, Valerie and Roy Harvey, Vernon Leonard, Ron and Kath Low, Edward Mace, Peter Mallender, Merville Matthews, Jim and Freda Nicholson, Alfred Richards, Gladys Sandercock, Jack Scar, Mr W. G. Seymour, Edward Sibbick, William Sinclair, John Strike, Robert Taylor, Lady Thatcher, Alan Thompson, Walter Thompson, Mr Tillman, Jopy and Harm Timmer, Richard Todd, Susan and William Topper, Mr W. Turner, Connie and Jan van den Driesschen, Mr E. N. Walker, Jerry

Warkans. Derrick Warren, Ellen Warwick, Squadron Leader E. Wass (rtd), Harry and Nora Watson, Dr W. N. Whamond, Mr M. Wilks, Nicholas Winterton MP, Mrs E. Woolfenden.

The undermentioned have also provided valuable assistance:
Judith Barnes (The National Sound Archive), Mr G. A. Coombe (The Scout Association), Mr A. J. C. Davis (The Ministry of Defence), Robert Garofalo (EPK Work in Arts, Bray Studio), Chris Mobbs (The National Sound Archive), Elizabeth Muenger (Command Historian at USAF Academy Colorado), Malcolm Oxley (St Edward's School), Mrs E. Parker-Jones (Penarth Local History Society), Mrs M. Perkins (Porthleven Old Cornwall Society), Duane J. Reed, (Chief of Special Collections, USAF Academy Colorado), Stephen Roberts (The US Embassy in London), Aileen Spitere (The Canadian High Commission in London), Mr R. Williams (Penarth Library).

Thanks are also due to the staff of the following establishments:
Public Records Office in Kew, RAF Museum in Hendon, Imperial War Museum in Lambeth and the Newspaper Library in Colindale.

My further thanks are to a very special group of people: Chaz Bowyer, aviation historian and author who encouraged me to write this book in the first place and who has spent many hours talking to me, suggesting sources of information, providing photographs and correcting my errors and my spelling mistakes! Without Chaz's generous help this book would not have been possible and I am in his debt.
My family for their constant support and encouragement in what was, at times, a difficult task. My parents,

Muriel and Reg Ottaway, looked after my dogs on many occasions so that I would be free to travel in pursuit of information and for this, and for their many other kindnesses, they have my thanks.

Lastly to Guy's own family; his sister the late Joan Stiles and his cousin Janet de Gaynesford. I was apprehensive about approaching them for information but they both unselfishly shared their memories of Guy with me, and welcomed me, not only to their homes but also to their hearts. I feel very privileged to have been able to call them friends.

Susan Ottaway.
Twyford, 1994.

FOREWORD
by Janet de Gaynesford

In asking me to add a foreword to her book about my cousin Guy Gibson, Susan Ottaway has done me great honour, though the honour is unmerited. I have so little claim to say anything about him that might be thought worth reading. I was the youngest and least of his seven first cousins; I know nothing of any of those personae of his – the bomber pilot, the war hero, the unhappy husband, the self-sufficient son – which most attract attention; when he died in 1944, I was only ten. And yet in spite of these limitations, I realize that what I did know about him was almost unique. Perhaps I saw a side of him that very few did. There are so many people who can assess Guy Gibson as a pilot, a 'hero', an efficient fighting machine. I knew him as a beloved brother-figure, inventing stories for me about a seafaring mouse; a young man of sensitivity and imagination, telling me that in *Hamlet* 'sometimes the words are so beautiful it makes my heart ache'. Many saw (and some disliked) the dedicated careerist, the ruthless commander; but this was the same young man whom I saw faint when some excess lighter-fuel which had spilled onto his hand suddenly ignited and flared up as he lit a cigarette for my father. And it was Guy who, exactly one week before the Ruhr Dams raid, remembered the birthday of a little girl of nine sending me a brooch of golden RAF wings. I think perhaps I saw him without a mask.

And so I am very privileged to offer this little foreword, such as it is, to Susan Ottaway's book. It is good to have such a detailed account as she has given us of his life, all

26 short years of it, the bad as well as the good, the failures as well as the triumphs. I believe he would be pleased. I know that I am honoured to have been asked to write this in his memory.

Janet Penrose de Gaynesford.
Porthtowan, Cornwall.
January, 1994.

PROLOGUE

Below the aircraft lay the German towns of Rheydt and München Gladbach. Both towns had been the subject of a very heavy bombing raid and, while the Mosquito circled for the last time so the crew could make a final assessment of the damage, the fires started a short time before had taken a strong hold over the buildings, crackling and spitting their destruction over a wide area.

Between the towns the railway lines on the main track which led from the Ruhr to Holland lay in a tangled skein. For the second time in less than two weeks the people had been disturbed in their sleep by the explosion of bombs that had rained down on the industrial areas of the two towns. Now the night was as bright as day with the light from the fires.

Up above the towns, in the relative comfort of their cramped cockpit, the pilot and navigator had one last look before turning their Mosquito towards the north-west and home.

Theirs had been a most successful trip so far. The pilot had acted as master bomber for this raid and in spite of a number of initial problems had been able to direct the raid satisfactorily. The targets had been well marked and the bombing forces that came in afterwards had dropped their bombs accurately. Now it was time to go home; back to their airfield in Lincolnshire.

Although he had been briefed to take a long route home via France, the pilot had decided that the shortest journey was the one for him and so it was towards Holland that he pointed the nose of his aircraft.

1

The pilot and navigator had not flown together before but, although this was their first trip as a team, both men were very experienced. The 23-year-old navigator was a Squadron Leader and holder of the DFC. The pilot, a Wing Commander who had celebrated his 26th birthday the previous month, had an impressive collection of ribbons on his tunic. He was the holder of the DFC and bar, the DSO and bar and, the highest decoration awarded by his country for valour, the Victoria Cross.

As they skimmed at low level across the tree tops, the navigator worked out the course the pilot would have to take to reach England and they both kept an eye open for enemy fighters and flak. Up ahead was the Dutch airfield of Gilze-Rijen which had been taken over by the Luftwaffe after the German occupation. Special care would be needed in this area.

Once the airfield was safely behind them, they flew on to the south of the city of Breda and then north of the town of Roosendaal. This would be the last town of any size that they would see before they crossed the coastline. The countryside from here on consisted of farmland and small rural towns and villages, occupied by the enemy, but inhabited by friendly, loyal Dutch people.

Approaching the small town of Steenbergen the pilot knew that something was wrong with his aircraft. The engines were making strange noises and their power was diminishing. Frantically pilot and navigator tried to think of some cause for this malfunction.

Below, in the little town, the noise had alerted some of the people not yet asleep and they peered out of their windows to see the black silhouette of an aircraft streaking towards them. It flew over the farmland to the south and on towards the centre of the town, between the two spires of the Catholic and Protestant churches. Some observers wondered why the crew did not bale out as it was obvious that something was seriously wrong.

From the cockpit window the pilot could see that if he

were to bale out, the aircraft would crash on the small town, so he began looking for a place to land the crippled aeroplane.

To the north-west of the town the buildings gave way to more farmland and, as he circled searching for a landing place, the pilot spotted a field. By now the aircraft was so low that the crew would not have been able to bale out even if they had wanted to. They were too near the ground for their parachutes to break their fall.

As they approached the field, huge jets of flame were seen belching from the backs of the now useless engines. The Mosquito struggled to maintain some height and remain airborne. One final arc of flame erupted from the engines before the aeroplane, the navigator and the pilot plunged to earth, disintegrating in a huge explosion that rocked the town.

The date was 19 September, 1944. The pilot was the man of whom Sir Arthur Harris was to say: 'He was as great a warrior as these islands ever bred.' His name was Guy Penrose Gibson.

ABBREVIATIONS OF ROYAL AIR FORCE RANKS USED IN THE TEXT

AVM   Air Vice-Marshal
S/L   Squadron Leader
F/L   Flight Lieutenant
P/O   Pilot Officer
AC   Aircraftman

Chapter 1

IN THE BEGINNING

Alexander James Gibson, Guy's father, was a Scotsman. The son of a company director, Charles Gibson, he was born on 14 May, 1877. He received his education at Edinburgh Academy, but he had spent many of his formative years in Russia and was a fluent Russian speaker.

When he reached the age of 21 he joined the Forestry Department of the Indian Civil Service. He enrolled at the Indian Engineering College at Cooper's Hill near Egham in Surrey, on 18 November, 1898. He was a bright, ambitious young man and studied hard during the three years he spent in the forestry section at the college.

His hard work was rewarded when at the end of his course he was offered a position in the State of Punjab as an assistant conservator of forests. He worked as hard in this new position as he had during his college course and quickly made a name for himself as a thorough, dedicated civil servant. Although he was very fond of the ladies, he had decided that his career must come first and would not contemplate marriage until he was well established.

By 1905 he had become an instructor at the Imperial Forest School at Dehra Dun, where he remained for a year, becoming deputy conservator in July, 1906. In 1908 he was appointed economist in Dehra Dun and in March, 1909, became deputy conservator and assistant to the superintendent of the Simla Hill States.

Life in India was pleasant. Alexander was, by now, earning a good salary and his cost of living was relatively low. During the first few years of his life in India, with no responsibilities except to himself, he was able to save. After ten years as a civil servant he was financially secure. His style of life was also pleasant. Had he been a civil servant in England he would, no doubt, have still been on a fairly low rung on the ladder of success. However, in these pre-World War 1 days, it was the British who occupied all the senior positions in the Indian Civil Service and their lifestyle reflected this. Alexander lived a comfortable life with servants and cooks to cater for his every need.

In 1913, at the age of 36 he came back to England to spend a holiday with his sister Nora, who lived in the Cornish village of Porthleven. He had, by now, decided that the time was right for him to take a wife. Since there were not too many eligible ladies from whom he could choose in India, the holiday provided him with a good opportunity to start his search.

One evening a concert was held in the old Methodist chapel in the village and he decided to attend. The choir included the pretty daughter of a local sea captain. Her name was Leonora Mary Strike and she was 19 years old. Alexander was not only impressed with her looks. She had a fine contralto voice and, as he came to know her better, he discovered she was also a talented artist. He decided that Leonora was to be the future Mrs Gibson.

Moving from his sister's house on the opposite side of the harbour, he rented two rooms with a family by the name of Cowls so that he could be closer to Leonora. Their courtship began, but did not always run smoothly as Leonora's parents were, at first, against the match.

Leonora's father, Edward Carter Strike, was the son of a fisherman. He was an ambitious man who wanted more from life than to follow in his father's footsteps. With his brothers he bought a small schooner and then joined the Hain Steamship company with a view to, one day, having his own command.

Marrying a local girl, Emily Jane Symons, he went to

live in a small cottage in the village. By 1900, when Edward received his first command, he and his wife had already had six of their seven children, five daughters and a son. The seventh, a boy, was born in 1902. Leonora Mary was the third of Edward and Emily's five daughters and was born on 22 September, 1894.

As Edward's career progressed so did his ambitions. He did not mix with the fishermen of the village and his children were not encouraged to play with their children. As soon as he could afford to, he moved his family from their cottage in the village to a large detached house he had built on the cliff top at Breageside.

Emily was, in her own way, just as keen as her husband to distance herself from the village life. Her daughters were always impeccably dressed and, when they went down to the village, would be in trouble with their mother if they did not wear their white gloves. Both parents took pains to show the world that they were successful.

Although they were a Methodist family, the four younger daughters were sent to Belgium to complete their education at a Roman Catholic convent, from where, their parents hoped, they would return as young ladies, accomplished in needlework, French, art and music.

When Leonora first announced her intention to marry Alexander Gibson her parents refused to give their consent. They considered him, at 36, too old for their daughter. He was obviously a man of the world, used to getting his own way, whilst she had only recently left the shelter of the convent. They were also concerned about his background. He spoke very little about his family and volunteered no information about his parents. They knew that he had a sister living in Porthleven. He also admitted to having a sister who was married to a British Embassy official and who lived at Potsdam in Germany. More than that he would not say. Throughout his life he remained secretive about his background and not even his children were told anything about their grandparents.

This secrecy worried Edward and Emily Strike and they told their daughter that she was not to see Alexander any more. Leonora was, however, a spirited girl with a strong mind of her own. She was flattered by the attention she received from this older man and his air of mystery may have served only to make him more appealing. Even after her parents locked her in her room and hid her shoes, she climbed out of a window and went to visit Alexander in her stockinged feet.

When her parents saw that, whatever their objections, she was determined to marry Alexander, they reluctantly gave their permission, although they still had misgivings.

On 2 December, 1913, at the Wesleyan Chapel in Porthleven, Leonora Strike became Mrs Alexander Gibson. Although her parents did not approve of the match, they gave their daughter a wedding to remember and one that was the subject of much talk in the village. Whether or not Leonora had forseen by this time what her new life with this much older man was to be like has not been recorded. Their wedding photograph shows Alexander superior and confident, whilst Leonora has the haunted look of someone who has just realized she has perhaps made a great mistake.

The wedding over, Alexander and Leonora left for an extended honeymoon in Europe, before sailing for India and their new life together.

Their destination in India was the small town of Simla, situated in the foothills of the Himalayas. It was an extremely pleasant place, built on terraces cut into the hillside and was the summer retreat of the European expatriate community when the heat of the plains became unbearable. The Viceroy had his summer home in Simla which had become, over the years, the hub of British society in India.

The Gibson home in Simla was a large house called Talland. Set in beautiful grounds, with many exotic flowers and bushes, the house was surrounded by a wide verandah and wooden stairways which linked the building with the garden below.

Leonora quickly settled into her new surroundings and made friends among the expatriate community. She became quite popular with the men as well as the women, a fact which caused Alexander to request a friend to 'keep an eye' on her when he was away from home. Leonora was beginning to discover that her husband was not the kind, considerate and thoughtful man that she had thought him to be back in England. In his own surroundings, where he no longer had to impress her, she discovered a ruthless streak that she had not known existed. He was no longer attentive to her needs. Quite the opposite. He expected her to attend to him and not mind when he continued seeing the women who had been his friends before he met Leonora.

This change of attitude was, of course, a great disappointment to the young bride but she felt that she had no choice but to accept it and make the best of her life in India. To go back to England and her parents would have been unthinkable. She had been so sure that she was right to marry Alexander and she could not face her family knowing how wrong her judgement had been.

Life for Leonora was not as bad as it might have been. Her husband's position had given her a certain status and his financial security ensured that she wanted for nothing in a material sense. She was not required to perform the sort of household tasks that would have been her lot back in England and found that her main job was to supervise the servants employed by her husband, to ensure the smooth running of the house.

In spite of Alexander's behaviour to his wife, he demanded of her complete loyalty and was constantly angry with her if he felt that she had given too much attention to someone other than himself. This frequently became a problem between the two as they often attended social functions together. There was always a dinner to attend or a garden party or a ball that would help to further Alexander's career and at times like this he was happy to have such an attractive wife on his arm.

On 23 June, 1915, when England had been at war for nearly a year, Leonora gave birth to her first child, a boy named Alexander Edward Charles. He was followed a year later by a daughter, born on 10 August and christened Joan Lemon the following day. The arrival of her children was not the only change to Leonora's family that happened during the war. Her brother Edward was killed, blown up by a German mine near Ushant.

Leonora fared well enough as a mother, but had very little to do with the care of her children, preferring to leave that to the army of servants her husband employed. Alexander sometimes took tea with his offspring but was uncomfortable with small children and regarded these occasions as a duty rather than a pleasure.

Apart from her pregnancies, the pattern of life for both Leonora and Alexander changed very little with the birth of their children. During 1918 an influenza pandemic was spreading throughout the world and India was particularly hard hit. By the time it had run its course the following year over 20 million people had died, worldwide, from its effects. In their remote mountain home Leonora and Alexander Gibson and their children suffered no ill effects, however, and on 12 August, 1918, the family was completed with the birth of their third child, a son. He was christened Guy Penrose on 11 September by the Rev H. J. Wheeler, minister of Christchurch, Simla.

Three months after the birth of the Gibson's third child the war to end all wars was finally over when the armistice was signed on 11 November.

Guy was a cheerful, chubby baby who quickly became the favourite of both his parents. As he grew, it became obvious that, while Alexander junior and Joan were serious thoughtful children, Guy was the clown of the family, always in to some sort of mischief. All three were cared for by an Indian ayah and other servants and it was only when their mother discovered that they were beginning to speak with Indian accents that she engaged an English nanny, a middle-aged lady from Portsmouth, Mrs Dunnford.

Their early years were happy ones for all three children. Although they were surrounded by the sights, sounds and smells of India, which were to be their first memories, they were protected from the poverty that they saw by their own privileged positions. They never knew what it was like to be hungry or to want for anything, except perhaps the attention of their parents. They were not starved of love, however, as their servants were devoted to them. Even the two servants who disliked each other because of their different religious beliefs, were united in their devotion to the children. On one visit to Lahore the Gibson family had so many servants that they took over the entire second floor of the Hotel Nidou where they stayed. It was to these servants and not to their parents that the children turned whenever they were in need of comfort or affection.

In March, 1922, Alexander was promoted Chief Conservator of the Simla Hill States, a position which often took him away from home. The Gibson's marriage had not improved in the intervening years and Leonora felt that she needed to get away from India and Alexander for a while. She decided to bring her children back to England for a visit and to introduce them to her parents and her sisters.

This was a happy time for the children, although it was at first strange to have only their mother to care for them. They quickly adjusted to this change in their lives and thoroughly enjoyed the time they spent in Cornwall. Much of their holiday was spent on the beach playing with their cousins, the children of their mother's sisters. It was here in Porthleven that Guy's love of the sea began to develop and he always kept a place in his heart for the little fishing village that had been his first experience of England.

All too soon it was time for the family to return to India. At Talland life continued in its usual pattern. Alexander and his wife grew more and more remote, but the children did not seem to notice. They would sometimes spend entire days without seeing either parent, but would always spend time with each other and became very close, especially Alexander junior, or Alick as he was called, and Guy. Their personalities were quite different but they got along very well with each other and Guy adored his elder brother.

In 1924 a plague killed over 25,000 Indians. Meanwhile, the Gibson's marriage was going through its final death throes. The couple decided to part and Leonora returned with the children to England, this time for good. The return sea voyage was very tiring for them all. The weather was dreadful and the children fought and squabbled constantly.

After many years of pampered living Leonora suddenly found herself in very reduced circumstances with three children to care for. Although Alexander initially provided for the family, he was not a generous man. Unable to afford to buy a house and unwilling to ask her parents for help, Leonora moved from one place to another until she finally settled in a suite at the Queen's Hotel in Penzance.

While the family were adjusting to their new life in England, across the channel in Europe an insignificant little man was being released from prison having served only eight months of a five-year sentence for high treason. While he had been serving his time he had written a book which he wanted to call *Four and a half years of struggle against Lies, Stupidity and Cowardice*. His friends persuaded him that the title was too long and he changed it to *My Struggle* or *Mein Kampf*. This man was Adolf Hitler and in the years to come his struggle was to have a great bearing upon the lives of all of them and especially that of the youngest Gibson.

Now that she had a base, Leonora decided it was time that the boys went to school. One of her nieces attended the West Cornwall College which, although primarily for girls, also accepted small boys as day pupils, and it was here that she enrolled her two sons.

Guy was by now six years old and had not had any experience of school at all. He settled in well, however, as did Alick and for a time life was quite normal.

Guy was developing into a confident, likeable little boy with a good sense of humour. He could be stubborn and determined, but he had a winning smile and usually managed to get his own way. He had a very lively mind and was easily bored if there was nothing to do.

One day in the lounge at the Queen's Hotel, Guy was sitting with his grandfather. The others had gone for a walk along the sea front, but Guy had had a cold and his mother wanted him to remain indoors. It was after lunch and grandfather had nodded off to sleep. Guy was bored having no one to play with and no one to talk to so decided to attract some attention by grabbing a big leather cushion from an armchair in the lounge and flinging it onto the open fire. He was quite unconcerned that he would be in trouble; he just wanted something to happen.

On another occasion at Parc-an-Cairn, his grandparents' house in Porthleven, Guy accidentally knocked over one of two large terracotta urns which stood on either side of the front door. When his grandfather scolded him for breaking the pot he deliberately knocked over the other one, breaking that also.

He amused his relations by his complete lack of shyness and by his self-confidence. He once told his aunt that now that he was a big boy he only used big words, like 'automatic'. His grandmother found that even when he used short words he could cause her great embarrassment. While taking tea in the hotel lounge one day Guy got bored with the adults' conversation and asked his grandmother if he might leave the table. When she refused and told him to sit still and keep quiet he leaped up on to his chair and shouted at the top of his voice, 'Granny's fat, Granny's fat'. Needless to say this had the desired effect and the entire family left the lounge in a great hurry.

Finding that child-rearing was a job she neither enjoyed nor wanted, Leonora decided that it was time the boys went to preparatory school, so places were found for them at a school in Folkestone and, at the age of seven, Guy became a boarder.

Earl's Avenue School, as it was called in 1926 when Guy and Alick enrolled, had been founded in 1921 by the Rev C. A. Darby, who was Rector of the small parish of Denton. He ran the school and his parish with the help of his sisters. In 1929 he changed the name to St Georges Preparatory school. As its former name suggests, it was situated on Earl's Avenue at numbers 23 and 25. The school has long since disappeared but the building remains.

The Gibson boys appear to have been happy at school. Their mother, along with Joan, had by this time moved yet again, to London, to a flat in Harrington Road in Kensington. Leonora did not see any necessity in sending Joan to school and kept her at home, saving the school fees. This was the beginning of a very difficult period for Joan as her mother had started to entertain gentlemen friends who regarded the little girl as a nuisance. With the breakdown of their parent's marriage, all three children had been made wards of court, although they were placed in their mother's care. When life became difficult for Joan she asked if she might be allowed to go to school and it was arranged through her guardian that she attend her mother's old convent school in Belgium. By this time she had, however, already suffered four years of her mother's indifference and neglect.

Guy and Alick had also been neglected by Leonora but they did not feel it on a day-to-day basis as had Joan. They went to school with worn clothing which Leonora did not think of replacing. When they were in London spending their holidays with their mother, she would sometimes forget to get them meals and she let them wander the streets, neither knowing nor seemingly caring what they were doing. Christmas was the worst time. Traditionally the happiest time of the year for most children, they had neither presents nor Christmas dinner to look forward to and could only look on in envy at other children enjoying themselves.

Their father did not help. He had remained in India until 1929 when he retired from the forestry service and returned to England to take up a further position with the Indian government, based in London. He lived in furnished rooms and the children would sometimes spend the day with him. However, space was cramped and Alexander had no idea how to treat children, not even his own. Although he never made any attempt to entertain them, he did, at least, make sure they were fed. Their meals with their father were usually picnic-type food, bought for convenience rather than taste and always cold. Visits to their father were not happy times and they often ended with Alexander feigning illness and retiring to his bed, leaving his offspring to their own devices.

Holidays from school were now the only times that Alick, Joan and Guy were together with their mother as a family. They often spent time with their relations in Cornwall. The children especially enjoyed playing by the sea and swimming in the rock pools by the beach. It was here that Guy might have first been called a dambuster. He liked to build dams of sand on the beach and when it was time to leave and go home would always smash his building efforts with his spade, much to the disgust of Alick who always wanted to leave them intact. The two boys also enjoyed cycling, although Alick had a lucky escape one day when he was unable to stop his bike as he approached the harbour wall. He was going very fast and shot straight over the wall and landed in the mud of the harbour, the tide having gone out. He was very lucky not to have been badly hurt.

As Guy became more proficient at swimming he also became more daring, eventually swimming across the entrance to the harbour and back again; no mean feat as the sea could sometimes be very rough on that part of the coast.

Now that Leonora was seeing men friends she had also begun to drink. She always said that she had been taught to drink by one of these friends, but what he had not taught her was when to stop. Sometimes she would get drunk and in this state could be quite unpleasant. It was then that her family suffered.

During a holiday in Porthleven Leonora threatened the children with a knife one night, turning them out of their beds and yelling at them to get out. All three escaped and spent a good part of the night in a field until Alick decided that it would be safe to return home. Afterwards their mother never remembered how badly she had treated them. Unfortunately for her, the children did remember and were understandably cool towards her.

After a holiday in Cornwall Alick and Guy were being driven back to school by their mother. Joan was also with them as she and Leonora were then returning to London. Leonora was a fast driver and drove a large Citröen. Close to the town of Amesbury, near Salisbury plain, both front tyres burst and the car somersaulted off the road and down an embankment. The children suffered no major injuries, although all three were thrown out and knocked unconscious for a short time. Their mother broke two ribs and was trapped against the steering wheel. When Guy came round his first thought was, not for his mother or brother or sister, but for his gramophone which was in the boot. He went to the rear of the car and managed to get the boot open. Taking out his precious possession he found a record, wound up the gramophone and started to play it, delighted that it had not been broken.

He was to be disappointed later, however, when it was stolen along with all the other luggage after Leonora had been taken off to hospital and the boys had been sent on to school by train.

By her own actions Leonora had lost what little affection her sons felt for her. The fact that Guy, who was her favourite, was more concerned about his gramophone than his mother must have hit her hard. However, she had no one but herself to blame and in the years to come her drunken behaviour would often be a source of embarrassment to her family.

Guy never really forgave her for the way she treated him during his early years and cut himself off from his mother as much as he could. To her credit Leonora did not entirely abandon her family but she had lost their respect, something she was never able to regain. It was a lasting sadness to the Strike family that their pretty, talented daughter should have sunk to such depths and had seemingly been unable to salvage anything of her earlier life.

In 1930 Alick left St George's prep school and went to Oxford as a student at St Edward's School. Alexander provided some of the money needed for the school fees, but Leonora was always left short of adequate funds and sometimes tried to keep Alick at home to save paying them. When she got into difficulties she was helped by her brother-in-law, John, the husband of her sister Gwennie. It was John who helped her again when her second son left St George's and went to join his brother at St Edward's.

In the same month that Guy left St George's, the Nazi party in Germany had been fighting an election. They emerged as the winners of 230 seats which made them the biggest party in the Reichstag and was a great victory for their leader, Adolf Hitler.

Chapter 2

SCHOOLDAYS

In September, 1932, Guy joined his brother Alick at St Edward's School in Oxford. At the age of 14 he was beginning to realize that money and well-known names could sometimes open doors that might otherwise have remained closed. He was, therefore, disappointed that he could not attend a school with a more prestigious name. The choice of St Edward's, however, proved to be an excellent one and Guy spent four happy, stable years here, learning not only academic subjects but decent principles and the art of playing in a team. In spite of his initial chagrin he always looked back, at his time at 'Teddies' with great affection.

The school had been founded in 1863 by the Rev. Thomas Chamberlain and was housed initially in a stone building at 29, New Inn Hall Street. As the school began to grow, the premises quickly became too small and in 1873 five acres of land were purchased in Summertown from the Rev. Canon Bull and plans were drawn up for a new school building. This was completed in August, 1873 and is the site of the present school.

It was the aim of the Rev. Chamberlain to provide an all-round education combined with strong religious teaching. He said that he wanted 'to place within the reach of parents of moderate means a school where their children could be brought up in the true principles of the Church, and have at the same time all the advantages of a Public School.'

St Edward's School in 1932 was under the care of the Rev. Henry Ewing Kendall. He had become Warden in

January, 1925, and during his reign, which ended with his retirement in the summer of 1954, the school continued to prosper. More land was bought, more buildings were erected, electric light was installed, shower blocks were fitted and a tunnel was constructed under the Woodstock Road, linking the quadrangle with the playing fields opposite.

Warden Kendall's contribution to St Edward's School was, however, much more than new buildings and an improved bank balance. He was a kind man whose first concern was always for the welfare of his boys. He was one of that rare breed who could make a person feel that they were important just by the way he spoke to them. No one was too small or too insignificant; he had time for everyone. His study was usually a mess, his desk piled high with an assortment of papers, but he got things done. He treated the boys with affection and they, in turn, loved and respected him. His slight eccentricities only served to endear him more to both boys and masters.

When Guy arrived at the school in 1932 he was installed in Cowell House, where his housemaster was A. F. 'Freddie' Yorke. He was an outstanding housemaster and it has been said that 'Cowell's under Freddie Yorke was one of the best houses in any school at any time.' Alexander Gibson was to say of Guy in a letter to Warden Kendall in 1946 that 'He always spoke affectionately of Freddie Yorke, his housemaster, and Guy owed much to him and the school generally, for his early years were not happy ones and I could do so little to help.' A strange statement from the man who, not only did nothing to help but had, in part at least, been instrumental in causing the unhappiness, not only of Guy, but of Alick and Joan as well.

With a father so lacking in most of the qualities needed by a boy in his important years of development, Guy turned to his teachers for role models and was extremely fortunate to find himself in the care of such dedicated men as Warden Kendall and Freddie Yorke.

Another of the leading personalities of the RAF during the Second World War, Douglas Bader, was also educated at St Edward's School. Older than Guy, he too was in Cowell House with Freddie Yorke as his housemaster. Like Guy, his family background had been in India and he also looked to Warden Kendall as a role model, his own father having died in 1922, the year before Douglas won his scholarship to St Edward's.

At first Guy had no one but Warden Kendall and Freddie Yorke to care for him. When he had been a new boy at St George's Alick had also been there and the two were drawn together not only by their natural affection for each other but also by their common circumstances. The entry into St Edward's was somewhat different. Alick had already been a pupil for two years when Guy arrived and although the two brothers were to remain close throughout their lives, at this point Alick was well established, with his own circle of friends. Guy desperately wanted to belong; he wanted to form relationships that would, perhaps, make up for the lack of a normal family life and so he tried to make friends by attaching himself to some of the other boys. This unfortunately, had the reverse effect. The other boys disliked him 'sucking up' to them and at first he was very unpopular. Gradually he changed his attitude and when he started behaving in a manner that the other boys regarded as normal they accepted him as a friend. In time he became quite popular, although he never inspired any hero worship from the younger boys. Even at this young age Guy had the ability to think through a problem and come up with a solution in a logical manner. He had, of course, been upset at his unpopularity but instead of sinking into a depression he set about finding a way to rectify the situation. He did not seem to hold any grudges against the boys who had initially disliked him.

Academically, Guy was an average student. He did not excel in any particular subject, but he tried hard in them all. He was most interested in science, but he also had a love of literature. He read all kinds of books and had a particular liking for Shakespeare. His favourite play was *Hamlet* although he could quote from many of the others. He also enjoyed the Arthurian legends. Years after leaving St Edward's, when he was already famous, a series of publicity photos was taken of him. One picture shows Guy sitting in a poppy field reading a book. The book, which had been given to him by his uncle, was Mallory's *Morte d'Arthur*.

Music had begun to be important to Guy. He especially enjoyed Wagner, although his sister remembers that he was also fond of Henry Hall and his dance orchestra. He was in the washroom one evening with his friend Terence Henderson. As they washed the two boys sang out the tune of the *Ride of the Valkyrie* and Guy beat out the rhythm with his hand, on the metal side of the shower. Freddie Yorke appeared suddenly and told them it was time to go to bed. Guy's only comment on this lack of appreciation of his musical talent by his housemaster was, 'Well, he never did like music!'

Sport played a big part in the life of a St Edward's schoolboy and Guy was no exception. Cricket, hockey, shooting, squash, tennis and rugby were all available to him and, it seems, he played a fairly good game of rugby. His contemporary, Bob Willans, remembers that Guy was often to be found in the middle of the scrum. He was skilled enough in the game to be picked for the school 2nd XV. Again, as with academic subjects, Guy was not exceptional in any sport but he was a trier. He threw himself wholeheartedly into whatever he was doing, be it school work, sport or one of his hobbies which included photography and cinema organs. His interest in the latter has never been fully explained, but he apparently became quite an authority on their workings.

Since all Guy's schoolfriends were boarders he did not feel at a disadvantage to anyone. No one had to know about his strange family life and when some of the boys mistakenly thought that his parents were still together and living in India, Guy did nothing to dispel the myth. He did not want to be the odd one out amongst his friends. During early teen years it is so important to conform. Freddie Yorke and Warden Kendall did their best to shield both the Gibson boys from any embarrassing situations brought about by their broken home. When Leonora's increasingly unorthodox behaviour led her to have brushes with the law it was Mr Yorke who spotted the newspaper reports and kept them from the boys. He knew how upset they would have been if any of their friends had discovered that their mother had been found drunk at the wheel of her car. It was not always possible to shield them completely from their mother's behaviour and some of their friends discovered that there were skeletons in the Gibson cupboard. One of Guy's contemporaries said many years later that he had the impression that Guy's mother had been a drug addict. There is, however, no evidence to suggest that she was addicted to anything other than alcohol.

During term time this state of affairs did not matter very much, but when it came to the school holidays there arose the problem of what to do with Alick and Guy. Sometimes they spent their free time with one or two of the other boys whose families were working abroad. This was usually at the home of one of the masters, Mr McMichael. At other times they went to stay with schoolfriends and their parents.

Sometimes Guy's aunt and uncle, Gwennie and John Christopher, would assume the role of parents and attend school functions. They also gave Guy a room at their house in Wales where he occasionally spent his school holidays. It was here that he kept his collection of Biggles books. The room remained his for as long as his aunt and uncle had the house and they always welcomed him to their home.

Aunt Gwennie was, in Guy's opinion, a 'wizard' aunt. He was also very fond of her husband John, a quiet, cultured man who always had time for Guy and would spend hours talking to him, discussing his hopes and fears and generally being the father to him that Alexander had never been.

In 1935 Aunt Gwennie and Uncle John took Guy with their baby daughter, Janet, for a holiday to Sennen in Cornwall. They rented a small cottage on the quayside and, in spite of the dreadful weather, had a wonderful time. Guy especially enjoyed being back in Cornwall beside the sea he loved so much and spent many happy hours with his uncle walking over the cliffs and watching the huge waves crash down on the rocks.

During the Easter holidays of 1935 Guy went with his housemaster, Freddie Yorke, and a schoolfriend, K. V. Calder, on a trip to St Peter Port in Guernsey. The trip did not prove to be an enjoyable time for Guy. He survived the ferry trip without a hint of seasickness, only to be confined to his hotel room for much of the visit, suffering from a migraine.

As his children grew older, Alexander Gibson decided that it was time that he provided a family home for them. His belated attempt at being a proper father to them was only partially successful. The place that he chose for this family home was Saundersfoot in Wales. The choice of location was decided because Alexander wanted to be near to a particular lady, with whom he had formed a relationship and by whom he had a daughter. He bought a bungalow called Summerhill and for a time his children came to visit him there. Even though they were no longer children, but, rather, young adults, Alexander still had difficulties in relating to them. He did not behave like a father and they knew him only as a cold, undemonstrative man.

Saundersfoot was, however, the ideal location for a house and Guy enjoyed being by the sea again. His father used to swim every day and provided a comic picture for anyone walking along the beach. He swam with his head well out of the water and on it he always wore a trilby hat.

Guy had always loved animals and was especially pleased when his father bought a spaniel called Wags. Alexander, however, did not like any show of affection and told his sons and daughter that the dog was there to guard the house and should not be fussed over. In spite of this Wags often succeeded in climbing into bed with one or the other of them. His triumph over Alexander was, however, always short-lived as when Alexander came looking for him he gave himself away by wagging his tail under the bed covers.

In spite of the fact that it was a very sombre household, Guy did not mind his visits to Saundersfoot, as he made lots of friends in the area. Of the three young Gibsons, Guy was the one who most tried to understand his father. He told the others that he thought that his father was basically a good man although he never felt the affection for him that he had for his uncle John. His tolerance of his father may have stemmed from the fact that Guy was Alexander's favourite and as such he was probably treated a little better than Alick or Joan.

Holidays spent with Leonora were hardly any better than those with their father. She always started out with good intentions but somehow became side-tracked along the way. One year she took Alick, Joan and Guy for a trip to St Malo in France. What could have been a good holiday turned into a time of boredom as Leonora went off to shop for clothes for herself and left the children to entertain themselves. With no money and only a smattering of school French there was not much they could do. It did not seem to occur to Leonora that it might be a good idea to buy clothes for them all. The boys often had to

wear threadbare shirts and trousers to school and Joan
had never been given the opportunity to choose any
pretty dresses for herself. Leonora did not wilfully neglect
her children. She was so wrapped up in her own concerns
that it never occurred to her that they might have unful-
filled needs.

Back at St Edward's Guy joined the Officer Training
Corps. His brother was already a Sergeant in the OTC
and Guy became a Corporal. During this period of Guy's
life significant changes were being made in Europe. In
1933 Hitler had become Chancellor of Germany, much
against the will of the country's president, Paul von
Hindenburg. He had no choice but to appoint him,
however, after rioting in the streets brought the country
close to civil war. The following year, when Hindenburg
died, Hitler took over and became president, at the same
time changing his title to Führer. There were those in
Britain who regarded this development as a threat to
world peace. Winston Churchill warned that Britain's
weak defences might lead to the country being 'tortured
into absolute subjection' should there ever be another war
with Germany. He called for defence spending to be greatly
increased and stressed the need for a strong air force.

In addition to joining the OTC, Guy also became a
house prefect, following in the footsteps of Alick. In
accepting this position of responsibility Guy was taking
the first steps in the development of his style of leadership, which was to earn him much praise and respect
later on in the RAF. Even those who would not count
themselves among his friends would always acknowledge
that he was an excellent leader. St Edward's required that
its prefects should promise to treat those placed under
them with fairness and honesty. In the service held for
the installation of prefects they were asked the following
questions:

'Will you be steadfast in upholding the necessary disci-
pline of the school?'

'Will you deal fairly and justly with those over whom you are set, not ruling by caprice or favouritism, but in sincerity?'

'Will you strive in all things to set a good and cheerful example to the rest of the school, remembering that your conduct is their chief lesson?'

Whether or not Guy obeyed all these requests as a prefect had not been recorded. As with all queries about him as a boy, the answer comes back: 'He was not exceptional; he did not stand out in any way.' Unexceptional he may have been to his classmates. Privately, he was weaving plans for his future which would ultimately prove him to be quite extraordinary.

Leonora Gibson was, by this time, an alcoholic almost beyond help. She occasionally remembered her parental duties and would sometimes attend school functions, but her illness made these visits times of great embarrassment for Guy. With the callousness of youth, he cut himself off from his mother and resolved, there and then, that his life would not be like hers, one of waste and lost opportunity. He was ambitious and was quite confident that he would be able to achieve whatever he desired if he set his mind to it and worked hard enough.

In July 1935, Guy entered for the Oxford and Cambridge School Certificate, achieving passes in English, History, Latin and oral French. With his determination to do better he re-took the exams the following December, this time gaining passes in English, History, French and Physics with Chemistry. Although his results had improved it was obvious that he was not destined to go to university and so he set about choosing for himself a career.

The 1920s and 1930s were times of great change, particularly in the field of aviation. In 1927 Charles Lindbergh made the first solo crossing of the Atlantic when he flew from New York to Paris. Lieutenant James H. Doolittle flew 'blind' for the first time, using only the instrument panel of his aircraft in September of 1929 and in November that year the first flight over the South Pole was made by Lieutenant Commander Richard E. Byrd of the United States Navy. In 1930 the British aeronautical engineer Frank Whittle filed a patent for a jet-propelled aircraft, although this was not to be tested until 1941. The year 1931 saw a new record for a round the world flight of 8 days and 15 hours set by Harold Gatty and Wiley Post and in 1932 Amelia Earhart became the first woman to fly solo across the Atlantic.

Perhaps it was the excitement of these achievements or perhaps it may have been the example of one of Guy's heroes, the First World War Victoria Cross holder Albert Ball, that led Guy to decide upon a career in aviation. Whatever the reason he decided he wanted to be a test pilot and he pursued this end with dogged determination. He approached Vickers and was advised to join the Royal Air Force to learn to fly. An application was made and eventually he was invited to attend for a medical board. This he did and was dismayed to find that, although he was fit and healthy, his application had been rejected due to the short length of his legs. He went back to St Edward's refusing to be downhearted and decided he would keep applying until eventually they accepted him.

School life continued, with Guy this time making a particular effort in sport with the hope that this physical activity would somehow stretch his limbs to the required length. He would not be put off the idea of joining the RAF and worked with steady determination at his exercises until it was time to re-apply. Whether or not these exercises worked one cannot tell. It is possible that, in the intervening months, he may have grown a fraction. Whatever the reason, when he applied for the second time he was accepted. The remark on his personal file read 'Satisfactory leg length test carried out.'

So began the first stage of what was to become such an illustrious career. It is doubtful if any of his masters could have forseen the heights to which he would rise, although

Warden Kendall did say much later that 'He was one of the most thorough and determined boys that I have ever known . . .' What Guy took with him when he left St Edward's in July, 1936, was a knowledge that, in spite of his unhappy family background, he entered this new phase of his life as a person of privilege. He would soon be an officer and would be required to deal with men of lesser rank. The lessons he had learnt at school would stand him in good stead in the years to come and he would not forget his obligation to treat others in a fair and honest manner and to lead by example.

Chapter 3

INTO THE BATTLE

When Guy left school in the summer of 1936 he had already reached his full height of about five feet six inches. His lack of height made him seem rather stocky but he was extremely fit. His light brown hair was inclined to be wavy and his eyes were of the deepest blue. A handsome young man, when he smiled he showed off two dimples and a set of strong white teeth. Already, in spite of his lack of height, he was beginning to turn the girls' heads.

His military career began on 16 November, 1936, when he was sent to the civil flying school at Yatesbury, in Wiltshire, having joined the RAF on a four year short service commission. Here his primary flying training began on Tiger Moths and Hawker Harts.

This initial training was completed by 31 January, 1937, when 39438, Acting Pilot Officer Gibson was posted to No. 6 Flying Training School at nearby Netheravon. The second phase of his training began on 8 February, 1937, and was to last until 4 September that year.

There had been a flying training school at Netheravon since July, 1919, when it was named No. 1 FTS. It had expanded greatly during the 1920s when it was one of the leading establishments for the training of Fleet Air Arm pilots. On 1 April, 1935, Netheravon was taken over by No. 23 Training Group and the school was reformed as No. 6 FTS under the command of Group Captain A. ap Ellis CBE. Guy commenced his training at Netheravon with 32 other officers and 11 airmen as No. 5 course.

The seven months spent at Netheravon were very busy for all trainees. The flying continued, using a variant of the Hawker Hart, the Audax, and Hawker Hind trainers. At the same time there were drill competitions between the different courses, parades, the annual sports day and even an exercise organized by HQ Southern Command in conjunction with the Air Raid precaution scheme, in which the station was 'blacked out' for the first time.

On 12 May, 1937, a ceremonial parade was held to celebrate the coronation of HM King George VI. It began at 08.30 hours and when it was completed the students were given the rest of the day as a holiday. More important for Guy and the others was the authority, received on 24 May, from HQ No. 23 Group for 31 of the officers and ten of the airmen to wear their flying badges with effect from 22 May. Guy was one of the officers so authorized and was very pleased with himself. His plans really were beginning to take shape.

On 4 August, when the flying training was nearing its completion, two of the student pilots were killed in an accident at Sutton Bridge in Lincolnshire. They were Pilot Officers P. H. Baily and D. L. P. Bagot-Gray. Although there had been another incident at the beginning of July this was the only fatal accident to happen to No. 5 Course and it had a sobering effect on the other students.

Guy survived the course without injury and on 31 August attended the combined Annual and Passing Out inspection which was carried out by the AOC 23 (T) Group, Air Vice-Marshal L. A. Pattinson DSO, MC, DFC. The Cup of Honour, awarded to the best officer or NCO was presented to Acting Pilot Officer H. G. F. Gaubert who achieved a pass mark of 85.57%. Guy passed with a mark of 77.29% and he was judged by his instructor to be satisfactory at ground subjects and an average pilot.

Having successfully completed his flying training Guy decided to visit his brother Alick, who had gone to the Manchester College of Technology to study electrical engineering and was now living in Rugby. He contacted Alick and arranged to meet him the following weekend.

However, on 4 September Guy received his posting and he scribbled a hurried note to Alick on the back of a photo which he used as a postcard. He explained that he wouldn't be able to make the visit as he had to go up to Edinburgh to join his new squadron. He gave his address as No. 83(B) Squadron, Turnhouse and said in closing, 'Tell you what it's like later.'

This was what he had trained so hard for and he was really looking forward to settling into his new squadron. He wanted to clock up as many flying hours as possible as it could only help him in his objective of becoming a test pilot.

RAF station Turnhouse was not exactly to Guy's liking. He wrote to his sister that it was rather quiet and there were not many girls about. His main excitement seems to have come from low flying, which was as much due to Scottish weather as to high spirits. On one occasion when Guy and his companion Oscar Bridgman were flying back to base from the north of Scotland, the weather began closing in and they were forced to fly very low. They managed to 'buzz' a sanatorium, frightening the patients who were sitting out on the verandas. Guy thought this was tremendous fun. These were still the days of the single-engine, biplane light bomber, 83 squadron having been equipped with Hawker Hinds. As late as 1938 these little two-seaters with open cockpit and a maximum speed of only 186 mph were still being used by many squadrons as their only bomber aircraft. Guy, being quite short, had jokingly asked one of his ground crew if it would be possible to extend the rubber pedals of a Hind with wooden blocks as he was having a slight problem in reaching them!

By March, 1938, 83 Squadron's stay at Turnhouse was over. On 14 March the Squadron transferred to Scampton in Lincolnshire and at the same time was transferred from No. 2 to No. 5 (B) Group. This proved to be a much more lively station than Turnhouse. It was very close to the

City of Lincoln and there was always something happening, although the parties in 1938 were not as uproarious as those held during the war.

Life on the squadron was quite hectic during this period, as many exercises and displays were held. Two weeks of exercises, held in conjunction with Nos 11 and 12 Fighter Groups, started on 1 April and the following month, on Empire Air Day, the Squadron took part in a bombing display at RAF Cranwell. The plan had been for the aircraft to display low level flying and dive-bombing techniques, but this plan had to be modified because of weather. The following day the weather cleared and the display was given at Scampton to visitors from the Observer Corps. In June No. 5 Group held its own exercises followed on 20 June by the squadron's temporary removal to No. 1 Armament Training Station at Leuchars in Scotland; they remained there until 16 July. The exercises in August were for home defence and in September the main event was the annual inspection by the AOC No. 5 (B) Group.

Whenever Guy had the opportunity to escape from this busy schedule he spent his free time with Alick in Rugby, or with his Aunt Gwennie and Uncle John in Wales.

A trip to his aunt and uncle's house was the closest Guy ever got to making a visit 'home'. For him it was the only place he could now call home as his father no longer lived at Summerhill in Saundersfoot, but had returned to London.

At Aunt Gwennie's he still had his own bedroom with his Biggles books and with the picture of Albert Ball hanging on the wall. Here he could really relax. His uniform would be discarded as soon as he arrived and hung up, not to be seen again until it was time to leave. Guy preferred casual clothes and felt most at home in old slacks and a roll neck sweater. If he had not been an RAF officer, his hair would have been kept a lot longer than he was now permitted to wear it.

He never minded what he did once he was with his aunt and uncle. It was enough to be part of the family again and he loved to spend time at their home with its large gardens. He could talk to his aunt and uncle as he had never been able to talk to his parents and it was to them he turned if he ever needed advice. This did not happen very frequently as Guy had very definite ideas about how he expected his life to progress. His childhood had taught him that it was no good relying on anyone else to fulfil his dreams; he had to take charge of his future himself.

It was during the time he spent with his family that Guy discovered how much he liked children. His cousin, Janet, was by now four years old and thought of Guy as much more an older brother than a cousin. When he stayed at the Red House with her parents she followed him everywhere and he never minded. She only had to lift her arms up to him and he would pick her up, whatever he was doing. He had endless patience with the little girl and spent a great deal of time playing with her or reading her stories. Perhaps it was because he remembered his own empty childhood that he was particularly sensitive to her needs. She was a quiet, shy child and Guy christened her 'little mouse', using this nickname when he wrote to her or sent her birthday or Christmas presents.

The games that Guy played with Janet were always exciting. He would drape a sheet over his head and chase her, pretending to be a ghost, while the little girl squealed with delight. He taught her to swim and in quieter moments would sit her on his knee and tell her stories about a mouse called John Henry, who found a child's toy boat and had many adventures in it. He told her Shakespeare stories in a very simplified form that she could understand and explained about King Arthur and his knights. All the things that had touched him and were important to him he shared with her. He never talked down to her, but made her feel she was very important to

33

him and she adored him. When his leave was over and he had to return to his RAF station she always looked forward eagerly to his next visit.

Aunt Gwennie enjoyed his visits too, as he always fitted in with whatever happened to be going on. He was not difficult to cater for and especially liked her home-made pasties. When she bought herself an electric toaster and kept forgetting to switch it off in time Guy even ate the burnt toast, saying that he preferred it that way.

By the end of October, 1938, 83 Squadron started to take delivery of its new aircraft the Handley Page Hampden. The re-equipment was completed on 9 January, 1939, when the Squadron bid a final farewell to its last biplane bomber. The Hampden was a much more sophisticated aircraft than the Hind. It was a twin-engined medium bomber of all-metal construction, powered by Bristol Pegasus XV111 engines and carried a crew of four.

Equipped with these new aircraft, the Squadron returned to exercises at the beginning of 1939. Guy was with them for only a short while, as he was admitted to Cranwell Hospital on Christmas Day, 1938, suffering from chicken pox. He confided to his brother that he was worried in case he had caught something really serious but discovered that childhood illnesses in adults are quite bad enough. Discharged from the hospital on 11 January, he then took 14 days' sick leave, returning to the squadron on 26 January.

On 20 February he once again left Scampton, this time to attend a navigation course at Hamble on the south coast. This lasted until 5 May and, although he passed the course with a mark of 81.1%, he did not find it a particularly absorbing subject. His instructor commented that he had average ability and could do well, but that he did not take the course or the subject seriously enough.

In September, 1938, Hitler and the British Prime Minister, Neville Chamberlain, signed the Anglo-German accord. This allowed Germany to take back the part of

Czechoslovakia known as the Sudetenland which was occupied mainly by German nationals. Chamberlain came back from Germany waving the signed paper and saying it would guarantee peace with honour. The following March the world saw just how honourable had been Hitler's intentions when he marched into Prague as conqueror of Czechoslovakia. On 6 April the Anglo-French-Polish military alliance was signed and Chamberlain pledged that Britain would stand by Poland should she be invaded in the same way that Czechoslovakia had been taken. This now seemed a distinct possibility as Germany was known to have an interest in the free city of Danzig, Poland's only access to the Baltic Sea.

It was, by now, becoming clear that Chamberlain's vision of 'peace for our time' was an unrealistic dream. Guy's lack of interest in his navigation course was probably due to his desire to get back to training on the Squadron. In spite of the more advanced aircraft they were now operating, the crews still had an enormous amount to learn if they were to be at all ready for the conflict which now seemed inevitable. They all felt that it was extremely fortunate they had not been sent to war in 1938 when all they would have had would have been Hinds with their pitifully small bomb load of 500 pounds and their very limited range. At least the Hampden could get to Germany and back and could carry a bomb load that made the trip worthwhile.

On 16 June, 1939, Guy was promoted to Flying Officer and as the summer wore on it became obvious that war was not far away. The Squadron continued training but they were to discover, when the war did eventually begin, that their training had not really prepared them for what was to come. The home defence exercises carried out between 8 and 11 August had illustrated exactly how unprepared for war they really were. Guy himself said of these exercises in his book *Enemy Coast Ahead*, 'This was my baptism of fire and it looked to me very cissy, just a few black puffs in the sky; but how lovely it was to be ignorant.'

In the middle of August Guy took some leave and decided to go to Wales. During the time that his father had had a house in Saundersfoot, Guy had made some friends there and had spent one or two holidays in their company. This time he had not arranged anywhere to stay, but on arriving had found a room with Mrs Thompson for 4/6d per day. He spent his time on the beach, soaking up the sun and sailing in a small dinghy. The evenings were spent with his old friends talking and laughing and sometimes on an occasional date. It was a happy relaxing time for Guy far away from thoughts of the RAF and the impending trouble. The only thing to upset Guy's peace and relaxation happened one evening when he was returning to his room having spent the evening with friends. He had to cut through a small wooded area to reach the guest house and while he was in the middle of this wood he suddenly felt that he was not alone and that someone was following him. He began to walk faster and faster until eventually he was running as fast as his legs could carry him. When he reached the road again he suddenly felt very foolish at having been so scared and stopped to light a cigarette and regain his composure before returning to Mrs Thompson's door.

The relaxing atmosphere was suddenly shattered by a telegram informing Guy that he was to return to his unit immediately. He hurriedly packed and said goodbye to his friends, feeling like a hero in an old war movie. One of his friends, Freddy Bilbey, was also on the move and the two shared the journey as far as Oxford, travelling in Freddy's car. Then Guy boarded a train for Lincolnshire. He arrived back at Scampton in the early hours of the morning to discover that Germany had invaded Poland.

For the next two days everyone held their breath while waiting to see if Germany would take any notice of the ultimatum issued by the British Government demanding that she withdraw her troops from Poland. By the time that it was clear that no action was going to be taken by Germany as a result of this ultimatum, a lot of hurried preparation had been made at RAF Scampton. Aircraft were towed away to far-flung parts of the airfield where it was thought they would be safe from enemy bombs. Gun emplacements were hastily erected and gas detectors were placed around the station. The ground crews were frantically busy whilst the aircrews had very little to do. Since everyone had been confined to camp there was not much they could do anyway except drink in the Mess. A lot of beer was consumed at RAF Scampton in those last few days of peace. Most of the aircrew of 83 Squadron would not be alive when peace once more reigned over their homeland.

At 05.30 on the morning of Sunday, 3 September, nine Hampdens from 83 Squadron were standing by to operate against the German fleet. There were two plans of action. The first was to be a low-level attack by six aircraft should the fleet be already in the North Sea and was designated Scheme B1. The six aircraft would be composed of three aircraft from each Flight. The second, an attack on the fleet in the harbour, was Scheme B2.

At 11.00 that morning war was declared.

For the next few hours the Squadron was standing by at an hour's notice, ready for action. A briefing was held during which it was impressed upon the crews that on no account were they to bomb civilian targets. They were given advice on taking off with a bomb load on board their aircraft. In spite of all their training the pilots had never had the experience of take-off with bombs on board and were anxious about the effect this extra weight would have on the performance of the aircraft.

The order to put Scheme B1 into operation was received at 18.00 hours. Guy was one of the three pilots chosen from 'A' Flight, the others being F/O Ross and S/L Snaith. 'B' Flight provided P/O Roberts, F/L Collier and P/O Sylvester.

At 18.15 the three Hampdens of 'A' flight took off. In the centre was S/L Snaith, with Ross on his left and Guy on his right. The aircraft felt very heavy, but all became airborne without problems and set course for the North Sea.

Bad weather had been forecast and this proved to be correct. Guy, flying with his crew of P/O Warner, Sgt Haughton and AC Hewitt, had no problem in keeping in the formation until nearing the town of Wilhelmshaven when the weather became so bad that he had difficulties in seeing S/L Snaith's aircraft. With the cloud down to a few hundred feet and the sea below growing increasingly rough it was, by now, becoming a very unpleasant flight.

Suddenly S/L Snaith's aircraft began turning and Guy realized that he was abandoning the raid and returning back to base. The disappointment was great. Having gone through the nervousness before take-off and the strain of a flight in such atrocious weather they all wanted to go ahead and make their attack, but it was not to be. Guy was very tempted to go on alone, but remembered the warnings that had been given at the briefing about breaking formation and turned his aircraft also. The bombs they were carrying were jettisoned over the sea and they headed for home. On the way home they spotted a German flying boat, a Dornier Do18, which Guy thought he should have a go at. However, when he called up S/L Snaith to ask his permission he received no reply and so had to let the Germans continue on their way back to the Fatherland. He was annoyed, as it would have been a wonderful opportunity to have claimed the first enemy aircraft of the war. In every respect this operation had been a complete waste of time.

Unfortunately for Guy and his crew, their problems were not yet over. By now it was growing dark and Guy had never landed at night in a Hampden. Flying around in circles over Lincolnshire they were lost for sometime before finding the canal that led them to the City of

Lincoln. Having finally reached a familiar sight, they had no problems in locating Scampton in the dark, landing at 22.30. So ended the first operation of the war for Guy.

While Guy was making his first trip of the war, his brother Alick was preparing to get married. He had joined the Royal Warwickshire Regiment and was stationed in Rugby. There, in her hometown, he met his future wife, Ruth. Although Guy got along well with Ruth when he arrived for a visit, she often felt that he would have preferred it if she had not been there. Alick and Guy were closer than most brothers and, once Ruth was on the scene, Guy seemed to feel that 'two's company; three's a crowd.' Unfortunately for Ruth, she was the third person who made the crowd in Guy's opinion. However, Guy was quite easy going and could be talked out of this chauvinistic attitude without much trouble. If he ever tried to throw his weight around, Ruth would tell him to shut up and he always accepted this rebuke with good grace.

Alick and Ruth had bought Guy a gold watch for his 21st birthday present and they gave it to him some weeks after the actual birthday. His reaction shocked them. He thanked them very much but asked why they had bought it as, in his opinion, he was a dead man. Even after just one operational flight, Guy had come to the conclusion that he would not survive the war.

The day of Alick and Ruth's wedding was 5 September. Guy had, of course, been planning to attend. He was to have been the best man. Unfortunately, the war intervened. With all leave cancelled at the outbreak of hostilities, Guy was resigning himself to the fact that he would not be able to attend when fate took a hand. The day before the wedding Guy spotted a dog in the Mess and went over to it to give it a friendly pat. As he did so the dog suddenly turned and gave him a very nasty bite on his right hand. The wound required stitches and was very painful. Wing Commander Jordan, the Squadron

Commander, decided that Guy should have 36 hours' sick leave. The timing was perfect and Guy was able to travel to Rugby for the wedding.

The journey proved difficult as people kept offering him their sympathies thinking he had been injured as a result of the war. It took him a long time to reach Rugby and his hand hurt. It had started to bleed again and the blood was soaking through the bandage and on to the sling he was wearing. Eventually he arrived at Rugby, just in time for the wedding, and had a very good time, in spite of his injury.

He arrived back at Scampton with a terrible hangover and the feeling he had, perhaps, seen his brother for the last time. No one knew what would happen in the next few months and now that Alick was in the army there was an even bigger chance that one or the other of them would be killed. He was quite fatalistic, but did not let the thought of his death trouble him unduly. He was not to know at this stage of the war that it would be many more months before he made another operational flight over enemy territory and that, for the time being at least, he was quite safe.

Chapter 4

83 SQUADRON

The first few weeks of the war brought boredom and frustration to Guy and the other crews. Although his first trip had not been successful, it had given him a taste for operational flying and he was anxious to get back in the air and do some damage to the enemy.

Arriving back at Scampton after Alick's wedding, he discovered that the Squadron had moved to Ringway in Manchester. Someone had decided that the aircraft were in danger of being destroyed on the ground at Scampton and that Ringway would be much safer.

Although the move to Manchester did nothing for the war effort, the crews enjoyed their short stay there. The local people were a generous, friendly crowd and the RAF boys were well looked after. Accommodation was somewhat primitive, but the fact that it was in a pub more than made up for that! There was hardly any work to be done, but there were plenty of parties with which to fill the time.

Guy, at the age of 21, had never had a serious girlfriend. He liked girls very much and they seemed to like him, but he had never thought about a serious relationship. Girls, to him, were for fun and not to be taken too seriously. When he drove past in his red MG their heads turned to look at him. Until then he had never seen a girl who made his head turn. Not, that is, until the one he met in a cafe in Manchester. From that moment he could not think of anything else but her and was heart-broken when she told him that she was involved with someone else. He would have tried to change her mind if he could, but his stay in Manchester was too short and he had to accept the hurt of unrequited love.

It was thought at first that the Squadron might remain at Ringway for some time and the crews were delighted at this prospect as they were really enjoying their stay. However, that proved to be a false rumour and the Squadron was recalled to Scampton after a very short stay at Ringway. The move was made worse by the knowledge that once back in Lincolnshire all they would be doing was night flying training.

Back at its home base the Squadron continued training in between abortive attempts to mount another raid against the German fleet. On 19 September 11 aircraft were standing by at four hours' notice, loaded with four 500-pound bombs. As the hours passed no orders to go were given and, eventually, on 20 September they were stood down. It was then discovered that 14 of the Squadron's aircraft had badly cracked engine bearer brackets and were unserviceable. That left just one servicable Hampden on the entire Squadron.

Over the next week the ground crews worked extremely hard rectifying the faults and by 27 September all the necessary modifications had been completed. Even with the Squadron back to full strength, however, no more raids were made during September.

Training continued during October. On the 6th Wing Commander Jordan left the Squadron, posted to 144 Squadron at Hemswell. He had spent only a short time on the Squadron, but was well liked. He was replaced by Wing Commander Snaith, a former Schneider Trophy pilot, who had been with 83 Squadron for some time.

As October progressed more attempts were made to launch another attack on the German fleet. Each time the crews prepared themselves, the aircraft were bombed up and then nothing. They would often hang around for hours waiting for the order to take off only to be told, much later, that the raid was off. This did their nerves no good at all and was bad for squadron morale. To alleviate the boredom and the stress of so many abortive raids they arranged parties in the Mess or sometimes in a local pub. These were noisy affairs in which the participants had a great deal of harmless fun. As the war progressed there were those who frowned upon the number of parties which were being held. Not being part of the operational scene, they failed to realize that these parties were only a much-needed, harmless way of relieving the stresses of wartime flying.

By the time that Guy was due for leave at the end of November, 'A' Flight had a new commander. Flight Lieutenant Oscar Bridgman was promoted to acting Squadron Leader and took over the Flight. This was a move which pleased Guy greatly. He had a lot of respect for Oscar and was delighted to be serving under him. Squadron Leader Bridgman was more impressed with Guy's capacity for work than with his actual flying. He considered him to be an average pilot and that Mulligan, Ross and Pitcairn-Hill were much better. However, when Guy was asked to do something, he never complained and later on when 83 Squadron aircraft were making many raids on Germany he never objected to being sent two nights in a row, as did some of the other pilots.

Guy shared Oscar's opinion of Jamie Pitcairn-Hill. To him Pitcairn-Hill was the epitome of an RAF officer and it was on his career that Guy tried to model his own. During the famous raid on the Dortmund-Ems canal in 1940, for which 'Babe' Learoyd, of 49 Squadron, was awarded the Victoria Cross, Pitcairn-Hill stayed over the target trying to draw the enemy fire away from the other aircraft and on to his own. His aeroplane was badly damaged but he somehow managed to get home, crashing on landing. He was not hurt and received the Distinguished Service Order for his efforts. Guy thought that Pitcairn-Hill's performance was the bravest act he had ever known.

Guy had friends amongst the aircrew, but was never

one of the more popular members of the Squadron. Some thought that he tried too hard and, as a result, appeared a little cocky. This was, perhaps, a reflection of his initial behaviour when starting at St Edward's School and was due, almost certainly, to insecurity on his part. By some of the ground crews he was regarded as being a 'bumptious little bastard' who could not be told anything. This was not, however, the opinion held by everyone. The LAC responsible for the servicing and maintenance of his aircraft at both Turnhouse and Scampton found him to be a modest, friendly chap who would usually buy his ground crew a drink if he met them in a pub.

A few days after Oscar's promotion Guy went down to visit Alick, who had by this time been posted to Coventry. One evening the brothers, accompanied by some of Alick's colleagues, went to the theatre to see a revue called *Come Out To Play* and starring Jessie Matthews and her husband Sonny Hale. After the show they went back to a party in the Officers' Mess, to which had been invited some of the cast of the revue. One of the dancers was called Eve Moore, a small, pretty girl with fair hair, to whom Guy was immediately attracted. They spent most of the evening together and arranged to keep in touch when Guy went back to Scampton and Eve continued touring with the revue.

Evelyn Mary Moore was, like Guy, the youngest of three children. Her parents, Edith and Ernest Moore, lived in a quiet road in the small town of Penarth, just south of Cardiff. Ernest Moore was an average adjuster with a shipping company and the family had a comfortable life there. During her childhood Eve had taken dancing classes and had been stagestruck from an early age. Although her parents wanted her to be a dancing teacher, Eve could not imagine spending her life in a small town teaching other people's children. She wanted something far more stimulating and longed for the bright lights and the excitement of city life. She made up her mind to use her dancing and acting abilities and make a life for herself on the stage. As soon as she was able she left home to pursue her chosen career.

During the 1930s she worked in a number of clubs until, in 1938, she won a part in a musical comedy, *I Can Take It* starring Jessie Matthews. The show was taken on a countrywide tour but failed to reach the London stage. However, her next part in *Come Out To Play* did take her to the West End. She was not one of the stars of the production but had small parts in five of the 28 sketches and appeared throughout the show as a member of the chorus.

By the time that Guy met Eve she had been in the show for eight months. He was fascinated by theatre people and fitted in well with Eve's friends. He and Eve also discovered a common love of books and music. After Guy's unsuccessful romance in Manchester, Eve seemed like the sort of girl who would help him to heal what he regarded as a broken heart. He also thought it would be nice to have a pretty girlfriend of whom he could boast to his friends.

When Guy next spoke to his Aunt Gwennie he told her about his new girlfriend. He explained that, since Eve's birthday was in December, she was a little bit older than he. His aunt was, of course, pleased for him and, one day, while speaking to a friend, told her about Eve. She discovered that the friend knew Eve; she had, in fact, been at school with her and could confirm that she was indeed older than Guy. When Eve had told Guy that her birthday was in December and that she was a little older than he was she had not told him that she had been born in December of 1911 and not 1917 as he supposed. The difference in their ages did not really matter to Guy, but he was hurt that Eve had not told him the truth.

By the latter part of 1939 Leonora Gibson was a hopeless alcoholic. She had not lived with her husband for many years but, although she had many men friends and her husband had many girlfriends, the couple had never divorced. Leonora lived in a series of cheap hotels and boarding houses, mainly in London. She had made several attempts to cure her alcohol addiction by spending time in nursing homes and in a sanatorium but these attempts usually ended with her discharging herself before the cure had had a chance to work.

In November, 1939, Leonora was once again in a sanatorium in the West Country trying to 'dry out'. Tiring of the place, she discharged herself and headed for London where she found herself a room in a boarding house in Kensington. There she remained for the rest of November and most of December. One evening, while dressing to go out with friends, she caught her dress against an electric fire in her room. The dress immediately flared up and, unable to put out the flames herself, she ran downstairs where the fire was extinguished by another guest using a wet bath towel.

Suffering badly from burns and shock Leonora was taken to St Mary Abbots hospital in Kensington where she died on Christmas Eve of her injuries and of pneumonia. She was 46 years old. When Guy's sister Joan took the news of her mother's death to her father he refused to come to the door and Joan was left standing on the doorstep while his housekeeper passed on the message.

The inquest passed a verdict of accidental death on Leonora and her funeral was held at Golders Green Cemetery. Neither of her two sons was present and Joan arrived late for the service, having been given the wrong time by her father who had arranged it. Joan believed that he gave her the wrong time on purpose. Even though she was dead, Alexander found it impossible to be charitable towards Leonora and no doubt hoped that all her children would miss the funeral.

It was left to Joan to dispose of her mother's possessions and it was a sad task. Leonora had very little to show for her 46 years. She had kept some of the things she had brought back from India, but when Joan opened the trunks she found that most of her mother's treasures had been destroyed by damp or by moths.

Although Guy had spent a little time with his father since joining the RAF he had not seen his mother at all after leaving St Edward's School. Since it was unlikely that she would try to visit Guy at Scampton, he had not needed to give any explanation to his friends. Whenever the others spoke of their families, Guy would ignore his parents and speak, instead, of his grandparents or his aunt and uncle in Wales. The photo he carried of his family home was of the Red House in Wales where he stayed with Aunt Gwennie and Uncle John. When he learned of his mother's death Guy did not tell any of his friends. He did not feel that Leonora had ever been a real mother to him and he could not forget the terrible moods and erratic behaviour during his childhood. However, since he was so reticent about his family it is difficult to tell whether or not he really felt her loss. It is likely that he felt a passing sadness but that it meant no more to him than the death of an acquaintance would have done. If he did feel anything more, he managed to hide it very well and on Christmas Day, the day after his mother's death, was enjoying a wild party in the Mess.

Alexander Gibson was not at all upset by the death of his wife. On the contrary, it came at a very opportune moment for him. He had been seeing a much younger lady and, with Leonora's death, was free to marry again. Eight months later, on his daughter Joan's birthday, he married for the second time, moving to his new wife's home at Chesil Court in Cheyne Gardens, Chelsea.

Whether or not the new Mrs Gibson knew of her husband's previous marriage is doubtful. On the marriage certificate he described himself, not as a widower, but as a bachelor and gave his age as 59 when he was, in fact, 63. His wife was 30 and came from a very comfortable background.

Although Leonora Gibson died leaving very little money, there had been a marriage settlement on her which, upon her death, reverted to her children. Consequently Alick, Joan and Guy were all due to receive a useful sum. Guy was the first to be approached by his father who, pleading poverty, asked Guy to return the money to him. Guy agreed and even helped to convince his brother and sister that their father's needs were greater than their own. How Alexander must have laughed at his children's gullibility as he took this substantial windfall to his smart new home in Chelsea.

During the late 1930s there was an American comic strip which depicted New York firemen in their fire station. The cartoons always featured a cat with a bandaged tail and a bubble, with the word 'Foo', coming from his mouth. This cartoon was the inspiration behind the nickname, Foo, of an ex-Halton apprentice called Lacey. His friend, Douglas Garton, known to his friends as Gerry, was a fitter with 83 Squadron.

One day Gerry was messing about in the barrack room. He had just been reading *Treasure Island* and was shouting '. . . at the sign of the Admiral Benbow . . .' whilst waving a broom handle about. Remembering his friend Lacey, or 'Foo', he changed this to '. . . the sign of the Admiral Ben Foo . . .'

Being something of a cartoonist himself, he decided it would be a good idea to decorate the aircraft and the following day he went out to Oscar Bridgman's Hampden, L4066, and painted *'Admiral Ben Foo'* on the nose. The idea caught on and 'Admirals' started to appear all over the squadron, including *Admiral Shicklegruber*, *Admiral Imaz Dryazel* (I'm as dry as hell) which had the Guinness toucan's head painted below the name and *Admiral Foo Bang*, the decoration on Guy's aircraft. Although Squadron Leader Bridgman was not too pleased with the idea, Guy loved it and took it with him to 106 Squadron later.

Nineteen-forty began with blizzards and heavy falls of

snow. The airfield was quickly declared unserviceable and no flying took place. Even worse, the roads around the aerodrome were blocked so it was not possible to get into Lincoln for some entertainment. With no pubs to go to there was a heavy run on beer in the Mess and before long the supplies had dried up. This called for drastic measures and an aircraft was dispatched from another part of the country to parachute some crates into the station.

During this period of inactivity the men were required to attend lectures on a variety of subjects, most of which they had covered more than once before. They were all getting pretty fed up and began to call themselves the 83rd OTU. The only high spots for Guy were when he managed to get over to see Eve, whose show was, by now, playing in the North.

After a month of boredom everyone was pleased to learn that they were being sent up to Lossiemouth in Scotland. Guy managed a detour via Glasgow to see Eve before heading further north to Lossiemouth. Upon his arrival he discovered that there had been some problems with the aircraft in the bad weather and that they were all unserviceable. For the aircrews this meant a pleasant few days getting to know the place and visiting the local sights, which included the local hostelries and their supplies of malt whisky. The ground crews were not so lucky. They spent their time fixing the unserviceable aircraft in conditions that were less than ideal.

In the third week of March the aircraft and crews who had been detached to Lossiemouth returned once more to Scampton. A week later Guy attended a Blind Approach course which kept him busy until 5 April.

The war was now seven months old. In spite of having made only one operational sortie, Guy had done plenty of flying. When doing airtests he often took ground crew with him and he had the reputation of being a daring pilot who often flouted the rules by flying very low. Although a number of ground crews admitted to being scared to death when flying with him, most agreed that he was an excellent pilot.

One day, learning that Gerry Garton had come from Scunthorpe, Guy decided to take him for a flight over his home town. They flew low over the River Trent, trying to see if a Hampden could be flown under the Trent bridge. Having scared a few bargemen on the river, Guy then headed for the town and made one or two passes over the main street. The next target was the steelworks and then, when Gerry was able to identify his own house, they circled it for a few times until his mother and sister came out to see what was happening. Mrs Garton later told her son that the King and Queen had been visiting the steelworks that day and that they seemed to have had an RAF escort. She was amazed when she heard the truth and learned that it had been Gerry circling her house.

On 11 April, after being inactive for so long, 83 Squadron was once more on ops. Two days before, Norway had fallen and the Squadron was sent to mine the channel between Denmark and Norway in the hope of preventing ships making the voyage between Oslo and Kiel.

Guy was in one of four 83 Squadron aircraft sent on 13 April to mine Middelfart. It was not a successful trip and Guy's aircraft was the only one which managed to drop its mine in the right place. One of the four aircraft, that of Flying Officer Sylvester and his crew, failed to return to base. Guy was accompanied on this trip by a pilot relatively new to the Squadron. His name was Jackie Withers and he acted as navigator for this trip. The weather was so bad that visibility was almost nil. As he came in low to drop his mine, Guy suddenly realized that he was almost level with the water and up ahead he saw the Middelfart bridge. There was no turning back. He had no alternative but to fly on and shot under the bridge much to the amazement of the mid-upper gunner.

After all the months of non-operational flying, 83

Squadron was now making up for the inactivity with a vengeance. On 20 April Guy climbed into his Hampden L4070 only to find it was unserviceable. He had to take the Squadron's spare and consequently was late in leaving for a raid on the airfield at Aalborg in Denmark. Jackie Withers was again acting as navigator and both he and Guy were amazed when they discovered at the time they should have been over the target that they were, in fact, flying over Copenhagen. The mission was immediately abandoned and they headed for home as fast as they could. Luckily they hit a fog bank, which was a very welcome sight in the circumstances and, hidden by this, they were able to get back to Britain, where they landed at Lossiemouth. It was later discovered that the compass in this aircraft had a 20-degree deviation.

At the beginning of May Hitler's forces invaded Holland and Belgium. The German Foreign Minister, von Ribbentrop, told the populations of the two countries that this was a measure to protect them from the planned attacks by Britain and France. On 10 May, as German airborne forces were seizing the bridges over the Nieuwe Maas, south of Rotterdam, Neville Chamberlain resigned and was replaced by Winston Churchill.

The week after Winston Churchill became Prime Minister Guy flew an operation to bomb the North German city of Hamburg, site of important dockyards and ship builders. The target for this operation was the oil tanks in the docks. When Guy and his crew reached the Hamburg area they could see that only one tank had, so far, been hit. They manoeuvered into position, then began their bombing run, diving steeply towards the tanks. At the moment that the bombs should have dropped, Guy pulled the aircraft out of the dive and began climbing. Something was wrong, the aircraft was heavy and climbed sluggishly and it was discovered that the bombs were still on board. Coming round for another attempt, they began a second bombing run and dived so steeply that they reached a speed of 320mph. As they came out of the dive the entire crew blacked out for a few seconds. Then they found themselves in the middle of the defences over Hamburg. Flak was bursting all around and Guy suddenly saw what he thought was a fire on the starboard wing. When he looked again he realised that it was a piece of metal flapping in the light of the ground searchlights and so looked like flames. At the same time he felt that there was something very wrong with the aircraft. The metal that he had mistaken for flames was, in fact, a length of balloon cable wrapped around the wing. In spite of this and the fact that the rudder had been damaged by flak, the operation ended safely back in England.

May and June proved to be bad months for the Allies. At the end of May King Leopold of the Belgians surrendered to the Germans and the British Expeditionary Force was encircled at Dunkirk in northern France. There followed the incredible rescue of over 300,000 men in an action called Operation Dynamo. Guy found out later that his brother Alick, was one of the soldiers rescued from the beach at Dunkirk and brought safely back to England.

On 14 June the Nazis entered Paris as conquerors and the following week, on 27 June, France surrendered. Britain was now the only country left to defend the western world from the threat of the Nazis.

While British soldiers were being lifted from the French beaches Guy had taken some time off to spend with Eve in Brighton. She was still touring with the show. They occupied their days sunbathing on the beach. The evenings were spent at the theatre until Eve had finished her performance and they could get away for a quiet drink in one of the seafront hotels. Before long Guy's leave was over and he was on his way back to Scampton. He was pleased to be going as it did not seem right to be spending time away from the Squadron. If the Germans continued to advance as rapidly as they had in the past few months, there was a real likelihood of Britain being invaded very

1. Guy's maternal grandparents Emily Jane Strike (nee Symons) and Captain Edward Carter Strike. (*Janet de Gaynesford*)

2. The three young Gibsons. Left to right Guy, Joan and Alick. (*Ruth Gibson*)

3. Seated on the steps of Parc an Cairn, his grandparents house in Porthleven, Cornwall, Guy hiding behind his mother, Leonora Gibson, his brother Alick and Leonora's sister Gwennie Christopher. (*Janet de Gaynesford*)

4. Guy scribbled on the ba[c] of this photo his own caption; 'Tarzan Guy after sunbathe last summer.' (*Joan Stiles*)

5. St. George's Preparatory School, Earl's Avenue, Folkestone, 1928. Guy Gibson 3rd from right back row. His brother Alick, 2nd from right seated. David Tomlinson 5th from right in front of Guy. (Tomlinson became a well known actor.) (*P. Tomlinson*)

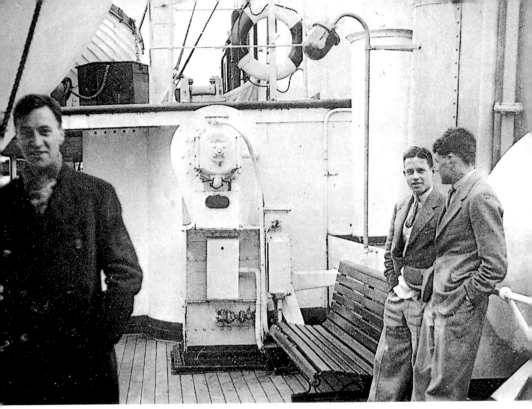

6. A school trip to the Channel Islands in 1935. Left to right, "Freddy" Yorke, Guy's housemaster, Guy and K.V. Calder. (*St. Edward's School Archives*)

7. Guy with his father, Alexander Gibson, and some friends outside his father's house, Summerhill, in Saundersfoot in Wales. (*Ruth Gibson*)

8. Guy's cousin, Janet Christopher, standing in front of her home, the Red House, in Wales. (*Janet de Gaynesford*)

9. Guy in the garden of the Red House. (*Joan Stiles*)

10. The wedding of Alick Gibson and Ruth Harris in September, 1939. Guy has his arm in a sling having been bitten by a dog in the Mess. (*Janet de Gaynesford*)

11. 83 Squadron at RAF Scampton in May, 1938. Seated in the chairs left to right, F/S Miles, P/O Ross, P/O Haydon, P/O Mulligan, P/O Gibson, P/O Pitcairn-Hill, S/L Snaith. (*Bill Sinclair*)

12. 83 Squadron. Standing in the centre is Oscar Bridgman. Guy is in the front on the left. (*via Chaz Bowyer*)

13. Trio of Hampdens over Lincoln Cathedral, 1939. *(via Chaz Bowyer)*

14. Guy Gibson with his Hampden. (*Janet de Gaynesford*)

16. Guy in front of his Hampden, Admiral Foo Bang. (*Joan Stiles*)

15. Douglas "Gerry" Garton who painted the "Admiral" cartoons on the Hampdens of 83 Squadron, shown here at RAF Halton in 1938. (*Douglas Garton*)

17. Guy's Hampden, L4070, after returning from Hamburg on 17/5/40 with a barrage balloon cable wrapped around the propellor. (*via Chaz Bowyer*)

18. Guy and Eve enjoying a day on the beach. This may have been taken at Brighton while Eve was touring in the revue *Come out to play*. (*Ruth Gibson*)

19. 23 November, 1940. Guy Gibson marries Eve Moore. Left to right Eve's brother, Dudley Moore, Gwennie Christopher, Guy's cousin Leonora, Guy, Eve, Eve's sister, Louise, Eve's parents Edith and Ernest Moore, John Christopher. (*Janet de Gaynesford*)

soon and Guy felt his time could be better spent than on leave.

On 1 July the German onslaught continued when the Channel Islands were invaded. That evening Guy took off on a raid against the German ship *Scharnhorst* at Kiel. He was carrying the first 2000-lb, semi-armour piercing bomb to be dropped by Bomber Command. The raid was not a success, however, as the release mechanism was faulty and the bomb fell away from the aircraft late, dropping into the centre of the town of Kiel. This was the first time that Guy had bombed a civilian target, albeit by accident.

On 9 July Guy's efforts and those of Jamie Pitcairn-Hill were rewarded when they were both given the Distinguished Flying Cross.

Guy was now due for some proper leave, not just the short time he had spent in Brighton. This time he decided to go down to Cornwall and asked Eve if she would like to join him. They stayed at the Wellington Hotel in Boscastle. The landlady's son was in the RAF and she had a soft spot for all RAF crews, even when they got up to outrageous tricks while staying at her hotel.

Whilst in Boscastle Guy decided it would be a good chance to introduce Eve to his family and so they set off in his car to visit his grandmother in Porthleven. Aunt Gwennie and Janet were also in Porthleven, staying at Parc an Cairn.

The visit was not the success for which Guy had hoped. Eve wore a pair of bright red slacks to visit Guy's grandmother. It was not the best choice as his grandmother was shocked to see her grandson's young lady wearing such brash clothing.

Guy wanted to take Eve to see his favourite beach but she preferred to stay with Aunt Gwennie and help with the tea, so he took his grandmother and Janet instead. Loe Bar, as its name suggests, is a bar of sand. On one side is the sea, on the other a freshwater lake. It is an eerie, beautiful place and Guy loved to go there. It was a disappointment to him that Eve did not want to share the experience with him, but Janet was delighted to have him all to himself and they left Granny in the car while they walked across the sand.

Soon it was time to leave Cornwall and Guy and Eve travelled as far as Bristol together before parting, Eve to go to Wales and Guy to return to Scampton.

It was depressing to be going back after a long leave away from the stresses of war and Guy felt even worse when he discovered that he was on ops that night.

At 23.06 on 24 August he took off with a new navigator, Sergeant Houghton, for the U-boat pens near Lorient. It was an uneventful trip and the mines were laid without any problems. After patrolling the area for a time, during which they spotted an E-boat and tried, unsuccessfully, to bomb it with a 250lb bomb, they headed for home. After a while an aircraft passed them, flying in the opposite direction. Guy was not sure that it was an enemy aircraft but turned his Hampden around and began chasing it. He caught up as he was again approaching Lorient and discovered that it was a German aircraft, a Dornier Do215. Manoeuvring quickly into position, the Hampden's guns thundered into the night and the aircraft plunged towards the earth, crashing moments later in a ball of flames. Guy and his crew were credited with a probable by Bomber Command and were all very pleased.

There was no time to sit back and congratulate themselves, as two nights later they were again flying, this time on their first trip to Berlin.

Although everyone had been waiting for a chance to hit the German capital this was not to be an occasion when any great damage was done. The weather was bad with strong headwinds on the outward trip and thick cloud cover over the city itself. Although they dropped their bombs there was no way of assessing the accuracy of the bombing, as nothing could be seen and the trip home was worse than the outward journey. All the defences had been alerted and the flak was very heavy from Berlin right back to the coast. Some of the aircraft ran out of fuel before reaching the English coast and landed in the water. Not all the crews were rescued and those that were spent an uncomfortable time bobbing about in dinghies in the rough seas. Everything considered, it was a disastrous sortie.

While the bomber squadrons were taking their destruction deep into the heart of Germany, the enemy were stepping up their pre-invasion plans. During August they began a series of very heavy daylight raids over England and the fighter squadrons were sent out to defend Great Britain in the conflict that came to be known as the Battle of Britain. On 20 August Winston Churchill made a speech to the House of Commons in which he uttered the now immortal words, 'Never in the field of human conflict was so much owed by so many to so few.' The battle was to continue for some weeks after this day and, while the fighters were defending the skies of Britain, the bombers were trying to ensure that the equipment needed by the enemy for an invasion would never reach these shores.

During September a series of attacks were made against the barges that were gathering in the ports of the occupied countries in readiness for the invasion. On 15 September 83 Squadron sent 15 aircraft to bomb the barges sheltering in the Belgian port of Antwerp. This was the largest force of aircraft that the Squadron had sent so far on a single raid and they were part of a large force detailed to destroy as many vessels as possible.

The defences over Antwerp were fierce and the crews had a bad time trying to stay out of the line of fire whilst making low-level bombing runs. Guy did not have any problems from the flak, but saw an 83 Squadron aircraft that had not been so lucky and was on fire. After returning to Scampton he discovered that the aircraft had been that of Pilot Officer O'Connor, a young Canadian pilot. His navigator and rear-gunner had baled out but the wireless operator, 18-year-old Sergeant John Hannah, had remained in the aircraft and had put out the fire with his bare hands, enabling the pilot to get the aircraft back to England. For this magnificent effort Sergeant Hannah was awarded the Victoria Cross and became the youngest airman to receive this decoration.

On 18 September 83 Squadron was once again flying over Antwerp. Guy delivered his bombs safely but had the distressing experience of watching the aircraft of his friend and role-model, Jamie Pitcairn-Hill, blow up over the target.

Guy came back to Scampton in a depressed state. Most of the boys he had been with at the start of the war, only a year before, had now gone. The final blow fell on 23 September when, after a raid on Berlin, Oscar Bridgman was posted missing. An SOS had been sent from Squadron Leader Bridgman's aircraft when it was over Oldenberg saying that one engine had been hit and then all communication had been lost. Much later it was discovered that he had survived and was a prisoner of war. He returned safely to England after the war was over, by a strange route that took him through Paris.

Guy did not of course know that Oscar was safe and he returned to England convinced that he would be the next to die. At that moment he did not really care what happened to him. All his friends were gone. Every one of the boys who had shared his experiences since the war had begun was now either dead of missing. Life did not seem worth living and even the thought of Eve did nothing to shake him from his depressed state. He managed to overcome his depression, and carry on, but he never forgot the men who had been such a part of his life. Once, when Eve asked him if he were afraid of dying, he thought for a moment and then replied, quite cheerfully, that it did not worry him any more as he would then be with his friends again who, he was certain, were waiting for him somewhere beyond this world.

Three days after Oscar went missing Guy himself left 83 Squadron. He was posted off operations and sent to 14 OTU at Cottesmore. He remained there for two weeks before being posted again to 16 OTU at Upper Heyford in Oxfordshire.

He was not happy at being removed from the action and requested that he be returned to operations as soon as possible. It had been planned that he would become an instructor on No 9 Blind Approach Training Flight, but this, along with a temporary transfer to RAF Watchfield, was cancelled and on 13 November, 1940, he was posted to 29 Squadron at Digby for night-fighter flying duties.

Chapter 5

NIGHT FIGHTER

Guy soon discovered that a fighter squadron was a very different place from a bomber squadron. There had always been a certain amount of rivalry between the bomber and the fighter boys and Guy was quite nervous about crossing over to the other camp. He decided, however, that whatever it was he had to learn it was still better than being rested. Having spent the past few months on operational flying, the last thing he wanted, was to let someone else have all the fun. If they would not let him carry out any more bombing raids for the time being, at least he could try to shoot down some enemy aircraft.

A flight on a bomber squadron was commanded by a Squadron Leader. On a fighter squadron the same job was performed by a Flight Lieutenant. Guy was posted to 29 Squadron on 13 November, 1940 as commander of 'A' Flight, having been promoted to Flight Lieutenant on 3 September. He soon found that his posting was not popular with the other members of the Squadron who had been hoping that one of their own number would fill the gap. Consequently Guy's first days on the Squadron were not particularly happy. The others, however, soon became used to him and his infectious sense of humour went a long way in helping them to accept him.

29 Squadron was, at that time, based at Digby, but they flew from Wellingore, a village south of Lincoln. It was just a landing strip in a field and was known as L1. The Officers' Mess was housed in a charming old country house called The Grange set in pretty grounds and yet

only a mile or so from the airfield. The buildings at L1 were primitive and had formerly housed a chicken farm. Even after its takeover by the RAF chickens were often found wandering around the field and the buildings. Although this gave the impression that they were working in a farmyard, it did have the advantage that there was always a plentiful supply of eggs to be found; a luxury in wartime.

At the time of Guy's arrival, 29 Squadron was operating Bristol Blenheims, but was in the process of converting to Beaufighters. He had very little time to get used to Blenheims, however, as on 21 November he went on leave. Accompanied by Pilot Officer Lovell, Guy flew down to Cardiff to be married.

Guy and Eve had become engaged in October and had decided on 23 November as their wedding day. Unlike many wartime weddings their's was quite an elaborate affair. Guy, of course, was dressed in his uniform, while Eve wore a wedding gown of ivory velvet and carried a bouquet of red roses.

The service, which was conducted by the Rev Thomas Jones, was held at All Saints Church in Penarth and was attended by members of Eve's family and friends. Guy's side of the church was almost empty. His aunt and uncle, Gwennie and John Christopher, were there but no one else from his family came. Even his cousin, Janet, was absent as she was confined to bed with measles.

Alick and Ruth Gibson had, in August, 1940, gone to Northern Ireland where Alick was stationed with his regiment. Their first child, a son named Michael Penrose, had been born in July, just before their departure. Unfortunately, it was not possible for the family to travel to Wales for the wedding and Alick was unable to be best man as Guy had been at his wedding. This duty was performed by Robert Shearer.

Guy's sister Joan had, herself, recently married. Guy had been unable to attend her wedding but did manage to send the couple £2 for a wedding present. Now Joan was unable to be there when Guy was married.

Guy's father had been married for only four months at the time of Guy's marriage. Having told his new wife that he was a bachelor at the time of their wedding, it was now rather difficult for him to confess to her that he was, in fact, the father of three grown-up children by his first wife and a daughter by his mistress. The easiest way for him to solve the problem was to ignore Guy's wedding.

After the ceremony a reception was held at the Esplanade Hotel in Penarth before Guy and Eve left for a brief honeymoon, spending the first part of their short break in a small hotel near Chepstow.

A few days after the wedding Guy was once more back at L1 and this time Eve was with him. He had found some accommodation in Wellingore but it was extremely primitive, a bed-sitting room with no washing facilities and a lumpy mattress. Eve was not at all impressed with these arrangements and soon after the couple moved to a room at the Lion and Royal pub in the nearby village of Navenby. From here Guy could walk the short distance up to The Grange, where the facilities were much more luxurious. The pub's chief advantage over the previous accommodation was that it had a bathroom. It was also the location for the village dance, held once a month in the hall at the back.

Thanks to the generosity of the local farmers and the fact that the airfield had been the site of a chicken farm there was always a plentiful supply of food at The Grange. This was prepared by two AC2s, Freddy Still and 'Taffy' Thomas. The former was a plain cook, but the latter had been a chef at the Dorchester in London and when he was on duty the food was excellent.

Guy went back to flying. During his brief absence 'A' Flight had been converting to Beaufighters and his first task on his return was to make himself familiar with the aircraft. The Beaufighter could be a difficult aeroplane to fly and was certainly quite tricky to land. During the first part of December Guy spent all his time gaining experience on the aircraft and eventually he was satisfied that he could fly the aircraft as well as any of his colleagues.

There were, of course, teething troubles with the new aircraft. Guy was not always very patient in handling these problems. One day he came back from a test flight in a roaring temper, shouting at the maintenance crew and demanding to know how he was expected to find his way around when the gyro was wandering all over the place. The long-suffering maintenance crew set to work and eventually discovered the cause of the problem. Having tested the aircraft again, Guy came back, this time smiling and telling them what a good job they had done. In his work he was a total perfectionist and expected everyone else to be the same. The fact that the maintenance crew had not been responsible for the problem was irrelevant to Guy. He wanted his aircraft to be in good order when he took it up, but he was not slow to praise the men if he felt they had done a good job.

Although Guy was undoubtedly a good pilot and, as such, was respected by all who knew him, he did not always enjoy their respect on a personal level. His behaviour towards others was often directed by his mood. If something was not as it should be and he was angry he could be quite rude to the people he considered responsible for the error. This was, however, usually as a result of his desire to get everything working properly and was not criticism on a personal level. Unfortunately for Guy and, perhaps understandably for those concerned, it was often taken as personal and Guy was not always popular. He once threatened to reduce a Corporal to the ranks for not saluting him. The poor chap had entered the Flight Office and had not seen Guy who was leaning against the wall at the far end of the office. This attitude did sometimes cause Guy problems, especially with the ground crews.

One day he was waiting to take off from Digby when he was startled by a fitter pulling back the canopy of his aircraft to tell him he still had to wait for a clearance Form 700 from the Flight Sergeant. He was anxious to leave and told the fitter to tell the Flight Sergeant to hurry. This message was not well received and a further message was dispatched with the unfortunate fitter that he would have to wait. Backwards and forwards the poor chap was sent until he finally was able to bring the missing form out to the aircraft. By this time Guy was in such a temper that he hardly gave the fitter time to jump down before he opened up the throttles and roared away.

In contrast to this somewhat intolerant behaviour, Guy could often show unexpected compassion. When, one evening, two of the ground crew arrived back at camp after having had a few drinks in Lincoln and woke up everyone, they were brought up in front of Guy on a charge. He heard their story, then gave them four nights' 'jankers', to show he had charged them. He then told them that he would give them a chit each night to say that they were needed for night flying duties and so they never had to take their punishment.

Another instance of Guy's sympathy for the ground crews landed him in trouble. As the aircrew had a little distance to go from the mess at The Grange up to the airfield, there was usually a truck stationed at The Grange to transport them. It had become a habit for the drivers to be given breakfast at The Grange while they were waiting to drive the crews up to the airfield. One morning when the call came the truck driver was still tucking in to his bacon and eggs. Guy decided that rather than spoil the chap's breakfast he would drive the truck himself. When the driver discovered what had happened he reported Guy to his superior for stealing the truck. He in turn reported to his superior until eventually it reached the ears of the Squadron Commander and Guy was reprimanded. Needless to say the drivers' breakfasts in the Officers' Mess immediately became a thing of the past.

Guy's first operational flight with 29 Squadron came on 10 December. That night there was a lot of enemy activity and three patrols were sent up. Soon after take-off he had a blip on his radar. In great excitement he began chasing the aircraft, only to discover 15 minutes later that it was friendly. Happily he had not been close enough to shoot.

The following night, while flying off the Lincolnshire coast near Mablethorpe at a height of about 1500 feet, he spotted a Junkers Ju 88 and began firing. Before he could do any damage the German aircraft disappeared into cloud and was lost.

For the next few days his time was spent in more practice, flying on a single engine and testing his radar. During a patrol on 20 December he spotted a Heinkel He111, but was unable to take any action before he lost sight of it. The following morning he saw a Ju88 shot down by AA guns at Manby and that evening caught a glimpse of an enemy aircraft in the searchlights, but was unable to do anything before it disappeared from view.

The situation was depressing but Guy was not the only pilot to feel this way. No one in the Squadron had had much success and they were beginning to wonder if their luck would ever change. Guy began to realize that the sky was a very big place and, even though he sometimes knew there were many aircraft flying around, he would go for days and nights and not see another soul.

The dreary operational scene was lightened somewhat by the parties organized by 29 Squadron members, which were riotous affairs. Even time spent in the Mess could be entertaining. Most of the aircrews had a 'Here today, gone tomorrow' attitude and were determined to make the most of whatever time was left to them. They got up to the same silly tricks that were being performed in the Officers' Mess in RAF stations all over the country. Behaviour such as forming a human pyramid, with the top man upside down, leaving his footprints on the ceiling.

One of Guy's particular friends on 29 Squadron was a pilot called David Humphreys. He, like Guy, was a dog lover and had a little dachshund called Fritz that went everywhere with him. He would sometimes stagger back to The Grange after a 48-hour leave on which he had been accompanied by Fritz and say 'If only that dog could talk!'

The police in Wellingore had only one representative, a constable who lived in a house just behind The Grange. He would sometimes come sniffing around The Grange, particularly the area where the officers' cars were parked. Since most of them never bothered to tax or insure their vehicles, if they spotted the constable they would immediately invite him in to the Mess and ply him with drinks. This usually had the desired effect of making him forget the purpose of his visit and he would return home quite happy.

Dave Humphreys and another pilot, Pilot Officer Graham-Little, were fond of shooting and both had air rifles. Having dispatched the constable back to his house after a session in the Mess one day, they decided to shoot the poor fellow's helmet which was hanging on a hook on his kitchen wall. This they accomplished from the back of The Grange shooting through the constable's open kitchen window.

The new year, 1941, brought very bad weather. Guy carried out only three operations in the entire month of January and did very little other flying. It was extremely cold and a lot of snow had fallen during the month, rendering the airfield unserviceable for much of the time; there were also strong winds which blew the snow into drifts and blocked the roads around the area. On 24 January the squadron transferred to Digby and operated from there until L1, or WC1 as it had now been renamed, was clear again.

In February it began to look as if things were picking up. On the 4th Guy took off at 18.39 to patrol the area around Wellingore. Twenty minutes later he was steered towards Mablethorpe and shortly after had a 'blip' on his radar. He continued searching and eventually spotted a series of flares. After nearly an hour he saw an enemy aircraft briefly lit by the flares, but lost it again as the flares went out, having only had the chance to fire at it for a few seconds. The Squadron Commander, Wing Commander S. C. Widdows, fared no better when, later that evening, he also had a blip on his radar but lost the aircraft before being able to fire on it.

By 6 February the weather had begun to get warmer and all the ground snow had melted. On the 9th only one patrol was sent out, this being Guy with his observer Sergeant R. H. James. Unfortunately they were out of luck once again, this time due to their radar malfunctioning.

On the morning of 15 February Pilot Officer Buchanan, nicknamed Jack by his friends, crashed while trying to land at Digby after flying his Beaufighter from WC1. He was killed instantly and the aeroplane was completely wrecked. Earlier that day Jack had been looking for one of the Mess waiters whom he had promised to take up for a spin. He had gone on a forty-eight-hour leave and was shocked to find, on his return, that this short time away had probably saved his life.

Towards the end of February the weather again closed in with more snow falling. Operationally the month had been a waste of time and it began to look as if March might be even worse. On the 7th at lunchtime a Ju88 suddenly appeared over the aerodrome, flying from west to east well below the low cloud. Everyone looked on in horror as the aircraft dropped four bombs which exploded between the hangars and the dispersal on the eastern perimeter fence. Miraculously, the only casualty was an aircraftman who needed treatment for shock. The aerodrome did not escape so lightly and substantial damage was sustained, particularly to the MT section, where some vehicles were damaged and others destroyed.

Suddenly the Squadron's luck changed. On the night of 13 March Flying Officer 'Bob' Braham shot down a Dornier Do17 and in the early hours of the following morning Wing Commander Widdows destroyed a Ju88, which crashed a few miles east of Horncastle.

That evening Guy was again on a patrol with Sergeant James, in R2250. Whilst over the Wash at about 21.25 hours he picked up a blip on the radar and spotted a Heinkel He111 about 400 yards ahead of him. As he closed in, he fired at the aircraft. A short burst was all that he managed, for, as he tried again, his guns jammed. Keeping the aircraft in sight, Guy treated Sergeant James to a performance of his entire repertoire of swear words. The sergeant worked frantically to free the jammed gun. As soon as it was again working Guy fired, this time hitting the Heinkel's port engine. Two further short bursts put an end to the starboard engine, part of which came off and hit the wing of the Beaufighter. Sergeant James and Guy were then able to watch as the German aircraft plunged towards the sea, crashing about two miles off the coast at Skegness. Guy records in his book *Enemy Coast Ahead* that he felt quite sorry for the pilot as he watched the aircraft crash. The next day he drove across to Skegness and picked up a trophy for the Squardron; the tail assembly of the Heinkel. For himself he took a rubber dinghy, the possession of which was to cause him some bother at a later date.

In the space of two days 29 Squadron's results had been better than anything they had achieved during the previous two months, and they celebrated with a party. The return journey from the party landed Guy in court. Having had a wonderful time, he was a little more reckless than he should have been and decided to remove the covers of his headlights. He had done it before and got away with it and he saw no reason why he shouldn't do so again. With Eve sitting next to him, half asleep, he shot off down the road, singing bawdy songs at the top of his voice. A figure suddenly appeared in the middle of the road, signalling them to stop. As he had done on the previous occasion, Guy put his foot down and swerved past the figure, missing him by inches. Unfortunately, this time his registration number had been noted and he was charged, not only with driving with unmasked head-lights but also with failing to stop and with driving with no road fund licence. When the case came to court he was fined £4 5s.

Having shot down his first enemy aircraft as a fighter pilot, Guy was again enthusiastic about night fighters and was eager for more success – perhaps too eager, as he had to be stopped from taking off one evening by the Squadron Commander, who considered the weather to be much below operational standards. Nonetheless, as soon as he was able, he was up again, searching out enemy aircraft.

On 8 April he was returning from a raid with his observer, Sergeant Bell, in R2250 when he was attacked from behind by a Ju88. As he made his landing approach the German fired on him and put his brakes out of order; the Beaufighter ploughed through a hedge into a field beyond the aerodrome. Guy was not injured but dis-covered when the aircraft came to a stop that Sergeant Bell had been hit in the leg. This was especially regrettable as Bell had only been attached to the Squadron from 219 Squadron for one week. Luckily the injury was more painful than life-threatening.

The rest of the month of April was spent with practice flights and the odd raid during which no enemy aircraft were spotted. When it looked as if he was settling back in to the old pattern of boredom, Guy made a raid in which he had ten blips on his radar and two visual sightings. He hit the second aircraft and was fired on in return, an event which he described in his logbook as being 'quite frightening'.

A few days later it was announced that the Squadron would shortly be moving to West Malling in Kent and the move had been accomplished by 29 April. This was a popular move for everyone in the Squadron as West Malling was not only in a very pretty part of the country, but it was also one of the front-line fighter stations involved with the defence of the capital. The crews were all convinced that their work would now be a lot more interesting than it had previously been and that their chances of shooting down enemy aeroplanes would be increased.

On 29 April he flew down to West Malling as one of a formation of eight Beaufighters. He recorded in his logbook that everyone was very pleased to leave, including the dogs! The Squadron Commander added the comment 'I agree.' He gave his own impressions of West Malling in the first few lines of Chapter 12 of *Enemy Coast Ahead*. He said that – 'of all the airfields in Great Britain, here, many say (including myself), we have the most pleasant.'

West Malling had, before the war, been the home of Malling Aero Club, but when it became clear that war was imminent, the airfield was taken over by the RAF and came under No 11 Group Fighter Command.

The station commander in April, 1941, was Wing Commander A. M. Wilkinson DSO. He held this post until June, 1941, when, on the 14th, he was succeeded by Wing Commander Widdows from 29 Squadron.

The Officers' Mess was a large, rambling house called The Hermitage. Formerly the home of an army colonel and his wife, it was set in very pleasant grounds along the road to East Malling.

Guy was hoping that he would be able to find more suitable accommodation for Eve and himself than in Lincolnshire. At first they stayed at a guest house in East Malling. This was called, strangely enough, The Grange and had formerly been a vicarage. One day Guy flew over The Grange during the afternoon when some of the guests were sitting out on the lawn, drinking their tea. He flew in low and when he was overhead dropped toilet rolls which unfolded and fell like streamers on to the startled guests. Since the house was almost hidden by large trees the staff were very impressed that he had managed to find it at all from the air.

After staying at The Grange for a few weeks Guy found a little cottage that was available to rent and the couple jumped at the chance of their first real home. Clare Cottage was in the grounds of a beautiful old mansion called Clare House. The house could not be seen from the road as it was sheltered by the trees and bushes in the large grounds. A driveway circled around the big house until it led, through a gate in the wall at the rear, into a courtyard. There, nestling in one corner, stood Clare Cottage.

The cottage shared a common wall with the big house but had its own entrance and was self-contained apart from the lack of a bathroom. The living room had a fire-place, as did the main bedroom and there was even a spare bedroom which was often in demand, especially after a dance in the Mess. The neighbours were friendly and allowed Guy and Eve to use their bathroom whenever they wished.

The time they spent at Clare Cottage was to be the only home life that Guy and Eve ever really had. For Guy it was the only home life he had experienced since he was a small boy in India. For the first time in his career he looked forward to coming home each day. He used an autocycle to get between the cottage and the airfield and Eve would listen out for its popping noise as it came up the driveway after a night's flying. This was the happiest time of their marriage and after they left Kent they were never able to recapture the contentment that they both felt whilst living there.

The crews, both ground and air, took no time at all to find the nearest pub. This was the oddly named 'Startled

Saint' built in 1940 within the bounds of RAF West Malling. Its name refers to St Leonard of West Malling who would, undoubtedly have been extremely 'startled' had he known that this once quiet place had become the home to many RAF personnel and their aircraft.

The first few flights that Guy made from West Malling were a disappointment to him. As with the flights made from WC1, he found himself unable to spot another living soul in that huge night sky. Then his luck began to change.

After a cold, cloudy day the weather cleared and the night sky was bathed in moonlight. Several patrols were sent up, including Guy. He flew around for a while not seeing anything. Then he was alerted to an aircraft in the area of Biggin Hill plot control. Shortly afterwards he saw the aircraft and fired on it. It proved to be an extremely good shot as the aircraft immediately began losing height and crashed into the sea west of Shoreham. It all happened very quickly and, although Guy was delighted to have hit the target, he was slightly worried that he had been unable to identify it before it disappeared beneath the waves.

He was not able to think about this for very long, however, as shortly afterwards Sergeant James spotted another aircraft. While he shouted directions, Guy manoeuvred the aircraft until he was in a position to fire. Suddenly, without warning and without a shot being fired by Guy, the aircraft crashed to the ground. It was discovered later that when Sergeant James saw the aircraft it had already been hit. Then moments later it was hit again causing it to crash. It was a complete mystery as to where the death blow had originated but it was certainly not delivered by Guy.

The Squadron as a whole was beginning to have more success and a few nights later, close to Beachy Head, Wing Commander Widdows damaged a Ju88, setting the starboard engine on fire. The damaged aircraft returned

70

the Wing Commander's fire and he was hit in the leg, but only slightly wounded. Two nights later Flying Officer Braham dispatched a Heinkel He111 near Richmond and Pilot Officer Lovell shot down a Ju88 into the sea near Ramsgate. Another Ju88 was destroyed near Beachy Head by Pilot Office Grout a couple of nights later.

These successes were a great boost to the Squadron's morale, but after 10 May the weather stopped a lot of patrols being flown and, in any case, there was far less enemy activity in the area. Further north, in Scotland, a German parachuted from his crashing Messerschmitt to land near Glasgow. Within hours this incident had made front page news as the authorities discovered that their prisoner was none other than Hitler's deputy, Rudolf Hess, who had allegedly come to try and make a separate peace with Britain.

At the end of June, 1941, Guy was promoted to Squadron Leader. Two weeks before Wing Commander Widdows had taken over from Wing Commander Wilkinson as Station Commander of West Malling. His place had been taken on the squadron by Wing Commander Ted Colbeck-Welch, who quickly became a popular figure. The Flight commanders were Guy and Bob Braham.

On 6 July Guy shot down a Heinkel He111. It was a clear night with excellent visibility. Guy was once again with Sergeant James, flying at 4000 feet, when the aircraft was sighted. After a short burst it caught fire and spun out of control into the sea near Sheerness. The same night Bob Braham destroyed a Ju88. Another good night for the squadron.

Soon it was time for a short leave and Guy took Eve down to St Mawes, Cornwall. He had decided that it was time that Eve learnt to sail and so hired a boat for the purpose of teaching her. He also took the rubber dinghy salvaged from the Heinkel he had shot down near Skegness. Eve decided very early on that sailing was not for her. She hated being wet and cold the whole time and would have preferred to stay on dry land. Guy, however, was having the time of his life. When he did come ashore there was nothing he liked better than having a pint in a pub with the local fishermen.

One day when returning to their boat they were stopped by a policeman who demanded to see their identification. Unfortunately this had been left behind at the hotel and so they were asked to accompany the policeman back to the police station. Here they discovered that a German aircraft had been shot down the night before and that, as yet, the pilot had not been traced. Seeing the German dinghy tied to the back of the boat the policeman had assumed that Guy was the pilot. Who he thought Eve was has not been recorded. Eventually, after much discussion, the couple managed to convince the policeman that they were loyal British citizens and were allowed to leave.

Life at West Malling was very pleasant. The local people were friendly and 29 Squadron was treated to their hospitality on many occasions. On Monday evenings Guy usually managed to ensure that his Flight was off so that they might go up to Ebbor House, the home of Glad Bincham who was later to become the International Commissioner for Scouts. Guy and Glad were to become close friends and many say that Glad regarded Guy as a son.

Guy and Eve were happy at West Malling. Guy was especially pleased to have the cottage and a family to come home to each morning after his night patrols. The family now consisted, not only of a wife but also a 'baby', a black Labrador puppy called Nigger. Guy loved dogs and Nigger was a real character. He became a beer drinker and no one's drink was safe with Nigger around. He followed Guy around everywhere, having drinks bought for him in the Mess and even going on flights with his master.

This part of Guy's life was probably the most normal time he ever spent, in spite of the war. The Gibsons made many friends in West Malling and their social life was enjoyable. There was always something happening and Eve, especially, enjoyed the fact that there was a flourishing dramatic society on the station. She took part in some of their productions, including one revue which was written by the wives and was entitled *The Merry Wives of Malling*. Guy, for some unknown reason, had a horror of Eve singing in public and made her promise she would not do so. She did not keep her promise and performed a little song called 'I'm a Divorcee' dressed in her wedding gown which had been dyed red for the occasion.

During the remainder of his stay in Kent Guy made many more night flights but did not add to his score of enemy aircraft. He was beginning to be fed up with what he regarded as an easy life and could see no point in flying night after night and achieving no results. His record, compared with many of the other squadron members, was good. For someone who was a self-confessed bomber boy it was excellent, but the real heroes of the squadron were Bob Braham and his observer 'Sticks' Gregory, who were having more and more success. In Guy's mind his inability to destroy any more enemy aircraft reflected on his ability as a pilot. He became more and more frustrated and poor Sergeant James often caught the sharp end of his tongue as he flew up and down on what he called 'stooge' patrols.

In spite of his dissatisfaction with his performance, his superiors were completely satisfied with Guy's results and on 16 September he was awarded a bar to his DFC. Although he was pleased, it did not alter the frustration he was feeling and he knew that he had to do something about it.

A visit to his old Squadron at Scampton convinced Guy that his real place was with a bomber squadron, where he felt he could be most effective. He was shocked, however, to discover that a lot of the bomber boys with whom he had flown the previous year had been killed. In the year he had spent with 29 Squadron there had been only one fatality due to enemy action, although there had been crashes because of bad weather. Even so, in his heart, Guy was not a fighter pilot and decided to concentrate his energies on being returned to a bomber squadron as fast as possible.

On 7 December the course of the war changed when Japanese aircraft bombed the American fleet at anchor in Pearl Harbor in Hawaii. America's entry into the war was generally welcomed and Guy was pleased, as he believed that the next step would be victory for the allies.

His final weeks were spent on a round of parties as 29 Squadron said goodbye, not only to Guy but also Bob Braham and Dave Humphreys. The final 'going-away' party began at The Royal Star Hotel in Maidstone. From there it transferred across the road to The Queen's Head and when that closed it was back to The Startled Saint until, at midnight, the party made its final move back to the Mess.

On Christmas Eve Guy's posting came through and to his horror he discovered that he was to be sent to an OTU and not back to a bomber squadron.

Chapter 6

FIRST COMMAND

When, at the end of December, Guy's time with 29 Squadron came to an end, he recorded his results as a fighter pilot in his log book. Between November, 1940, and December, 1941, these were as follows –

> Destroyed 3
> Probable 1
> Damaged 3

Although he could not be regarded as a fighter ace, he had done well during his time with 29 Squadron and his assessment judged him to be above the average as a night fighter pilot and in air gunnery.

The posting to an OTU was a great disappointment, but there was not much Guy could do about it on Christmas Eve. By the new year he was installed at 51 OTU, RAF Cranfield in Bedfordshire, as chief flying instructor. In his log book he recorded the move with the words – 'With the New Year I am posted as CFI to 51 OTU, Cranfield. This being held as a rest from operations!!!'

In those days there was very little training for the post of flying instructor. If you were capable of flying it was thought that you were capable of passing on the techniques to others. Guy was not impressed with the title of Chief Flying Instructor. It was not a job he wanted, nor did he feel he had any talent for it. And he certainly did not want a rest!

He determined to make a fuss and to keep making a fuss until someone saw the sense of his argument and posted him back to a bomber squadron. To Guy's annoyance this took a little longer than he had anticipated.

Since Guy had no intention of remaining at Cranfield for very long Eve had decided to remain at Clare Cottage, at least until she knew what Guy was going to be doing. During his first month at Cranfield he managed to get back to West Malling four times. On 12 January he flew into the aerodrome in a Westland Lysander with Dave Humphreys as passenger, the purpose of the visit being to attend a party which was being held at the home of Glad Bincham. Dave had also been posted to 51 OTU so there was at least one friendly face at Cranfield.

When it became clear that Guy's posting back to operations was not imminent, Eve decided to pack up and return to Penarth to stay with her parents. Once she had settled in, she found herself a job in Cardiff, working with the Red Cross in the prisoner of war department. Before Eve left for Wales, Guy managed to get back to Clare Cottage for one last visit and to pick up Nigger, who was going to Cranfield with him. An OTU was, in Guy's opinion, a very boring place and he found it unbearable without his four-legged friend and drinking partner.

Although he was flying a lot, he was bored and frustrated at being away from the action. He also disliked his work and told Eve that 'This instructing lark is driving me round the bend!'

In March he was ordered to report to Air Marshal Harris who had recently taken over at Bomber Command. Within days of this meeting Guy's prayers were answered and he was posted to Coningsby to take over command of 106 Squadron, and was promoted at the same time to acting Wing Commander.

The Squadron at this time was operating with Avro Manchesters, an aircraft with a reputation for being temperamental and unreliable in the air. A twin-engined bomber, it was powered by Rolls-Royce Vulture engines and had great difficulty in maintaining height with one engine shut down. It was definitely not a favourite amongst the aircrews. When Guy first arrived at Coningsby, he was met by a chap called Dunlop Mackenzie whom he had known on 83 Squadron. When Guy told him that he had come to take over the Squadron he was told that he was a clot as the aircraft were awful. The Manchester was withdrawn from service during June, 1942, but Guy made at least 16 flights before this happened, four of these on actual raids.

The Squadron that Guy took over in April, 1942, was a happy one and Guy was determined to continue in the same tradition, maintaining good morale and results. He looked forward very much to introducing some of his own ideas to the Squadron and expressed the hope that it would be as happy as 29 Squadron had been under the command of Ted Colbeck-Welch.

Guy was still only 23 years old. Short and stocky, he had an open, boyish grin and looked to many to be far too young to be a pilot, much less the CO of the Squadron. These doubters were, however, shocked when they discovered he could be quite a strict disciplinarian and was certainly no push-over. His lack of stature belied a grim determination to make his Squadron the very best in the Group.

His first contact with the members of 106 was at a dance held at the WAAF Mess on the day of his arrival. He was careful to remain sober, although some of the others were not. That way he was able to discover in the informal atmosphere of the dance what most of their gripes were.

The next day he met the NCO aircrews and gave them a rocket for failing to stand up as he walked into the room. With everyone now sober, the mood was quite different and Guy was able to tell them what he expected of them. Anyone who worked hard and gave his very best to the job would have no problems with him. Those who were not as dedicated to the task as he would find life difficult with their new CO.

Joining the Squadron on the same day as Guy was a Flight-Lieutenant Robertson, whom Guy quickly promoted to Squadron Leader to take over 'A' Flight. In *Enemy Coast Ahead* Guy describes 'Robbo' as a New Zealander. He was in fact, like his deputy Bill Whamond, from Bulawayo in Rhodesia and both men, in time, became quite close friends of Guy. The friendship with Robbo was not to last, as he was killed in July, 1942, while on an operation to bomb the city of Hamburg.

Guy's first operational trip with his new Squadron was a mine-laying expedition. These trips were referred to as 'gardening' and the areas in which the mines were to be dropped were 'gardens'. These were the sort of trips that freshmen crews were usually given, but since Guy had not flown on a bombing raid for over a year he decided to give himself a relatively easy return to operations. None of these flights were, of course, easy. There was still a danger from enemy fighters, but they presented less of a danger than bombing targets on land. In good, clear weather Guy with his crew of seven took off at 20.20 hrs returning at 03.30 hrs having successfully planted their mines.

Three days later, on 26 April, Guy flew over Germany for the first time in over a year. The target was Rostock and it was the third night running that this town had been bombed. Consequently the defences were much heavier than on the previous two nights. By this time bomber aircraft had been equipped with cameras to enable them to judge the accuracy of their bombing. The only problem with this system was that the cameras could not get a clear picture if the aircraft was flying at less than 4000 feet and at this height bombing was less accurate than at a lower level. Five aircraft from 106 made the attack at about 4800 feet. Guy himself dropped his bombs from 3500 feet and claimed to have had good results. The results overall were difficult to judge as there was a vast amount of smoke over the area which blotted out almost all sight of the target.

As the Squadron Commander Guy flew less operations than he had before and on the nights when he was not flying he could usually be found in the Ops Room waiting for news of his crews.

One night he found himself waiting in the Ops Room with the wife of one of the pilots. He described the incident in *Enemy Coast Ahead*. As she wrote the landing times of the aircraft on a large board on the wall, she waited for news of her own husband. Eventually it became clear that he would not be returning and Guy persuaded her to leave the room and let him take her home. He tells how close to tears he was himself as she collected from the WAAF Officers' Mess the meagre rations she had bought the previous day and then allowed herself to be driven home. Still a very young woman, this was the second time she had been widowed in this way.

Soon after Guy took over on the Squadron an order was received from Bomber Command banning wives from living within 40 miles of their husbands who were aircrew on a bomber station. This was an order which Guy felt was sensible. He had seen the strain suffered by both the men and their wives when they lived together off the station. If the wives were not in the vicinity of the station, they did not have the constant worry for their menfolk every time they heard an aircraft take off. The men, in turn, could devote themselves to developing a strong squadron spirit and not be constantly worrying about getting home. This spirit was essential, especially in wartime, as the success of the squadron depended so much on the interaction of its members.

Guy wanted to start a family now that he and Eve had been married for 18 months. He loved children and wanted to be a good father of the kind his own father had never been to him: loving and caring and interested in his child's activities. At first Eve did not seem to be too keen. Then she told him that she was unable to have children. The medical reason that she gave was not one that would, necessarily, have precluded her from having a child, but Guy found it hard to decide whether she was really unable or merely unwilling to be a mother. Whatever the real reason was, it was a bitter blow to him, the more so because Eve had not told him this before they were married. It marked the beginning of the end as far as their marriage was concerned.

On the evening of 8 May Guy set out once more for Germany. His crew for this operation included Pilot Officer Hutchison, who was later to accompany him to the Möhne dam in 1943. Their target was the Heinkel works at Warnemunde and it was, as Guy described in his log book, a hot trip. They carried six 1000lb bombs which they dropped from a height of 3500 feet and the opposition was fierce. The flight lasted seven hours and 20 minutes.

Three days later, on 11 May, Guy was admitted to the RAF hospital at Rauceby. For a long time he had suffered with sinus problems and he went into hospital to have an operation to clear up the problem and stop the headaches that he had been suffering. After a two-week stay at Rauceby he flew down to Cardiff in an Airspeed Oxford to spend 14 days convalescence there. Eve had managed to get some time off from her Red Cross work and was at the airfield to meet Guy when he arrived. They had a pleasant two weeks' leave and on 30 June Guy's friends Robbo and Bill Whamond flew down to Cardiff in the Oxford to fetch him back to Coningsby. He must have enjoyed himself as in his log book he noted his return date as 'June 31st'.

The Squadron was now converting to Avro Lancaster Bombers. These were similar in appearance to, and had been developed from, the Manchester. They were powered, however, by four Rolls-Royce Merlin engines and there was no repeat of the problems encountered by the Manchester. In time the Lancaster became the most famous four-engined bomber of the entire war and had a superior performance to any of its rivals, British or American.

Guy had had the chance of a short flight in a Lancaster before going into hospital. Then he flew as second pilot to Squadron Leader Stenner. On his return he accompanied his friend, Flight Lieutenant John Hopgood, who had had some experience of the aircraft.

On 8 July Guy's first operation in a Lancaster was made to bomb Wilhelmshaven. Of the ten aircraft to make the trip six located and bombed the target, three returned to base with technical trouble and the tenth failed to return. Three days later the Squadron made its biggest daylight raid to date when nine aircraft attacked the submarine works at Danzig. This was especially dangerous, as it involved a round trip of 1700 miles, mostly over enemy territory. It was undertaken in appalling weather and Guy's aircraft, arriving late at the target, bombed a ship at Gdynia, missing it by a very small margin.

On 25 July Guy flew a VIP party up to Coningsby to see, in his words, 'a crack station'. The party consisted of Air Commodore Clarke, Air Commodore Baker, Group Captain Sir Louis Grieg and the Air Minister, Sir Archibald Sinclair.

This was a trip which very nearly had an embarrassing end. The Air Minister was interested in the performance of the aircraft and two engines were shut down to demonstrate its ability to fly on only two. Unfortunately, when it came time to start them again, an error was made and the other two were feathered. Happily, the mistake was rectified before anyone noticed and before any further problems were caused.

Operations on other German targets followed until, on 31 July, came a raid which was described in the Squadron operation record book as one of the great events in the history of the Squadron. Twenty-one aircraft were sent out to bomb the city of Düsseldorf. Eighteen aircraft located and bombed the target in clear weather, dropping

63 tons of bombs. This beat the previous Squadron record for bomb loads, held since 25 June, when 19 aircraft had dropped 55 tons of bombs. The only aircraft which failed to return that night had on board the first 8000lb bomb ever carried.

During the month of July, 106 Squadron had made a total of 84 operational flights and had dropped a total of 239.7 tons of bombs. This was not only a record for the Squadron; it surpassed the records of every other squadron in the whole of No. 5 Group.

Guy's first command was shaping up nicely. Under him the Squadron continued to improve. He managed to inject into the others his own enthusiasm and determination and was beginning to be regarded as a very good leader. In spite of being a hard taskmaster he did have a very human streak and would go out of his way to help anyone, should the need arise. When the mother of one of his Pilot Officers died, he immediately sent him home to be with his family and lent him an aircraft to speed his journey.

Guy was the type of squadron commander who led by example. He would never ask anyone to do anything he had not done or could not do. Although he had the responsibility of the Squadron, a task he did not regard lightly, he still considered himself to be, first and foremost, an operational pilot. He never shied away from dangerous targets; in fact he did not feel happy about sending his crews on such missions without himself going with them. He may not have been universally loved but he had certainly earned the respect of his men by his dedication to duty and to them. Perhaps part of Guy's success as a leader can be attributed to the fact that he never allowed himself to appear nervous or diffident and was, therefore, in command right from the start.

This confident, outgoing attitude did not endear him to the ground crews unfortunately. Behind his back they referred to him as 'the boy emperor', and he was not usually a popular figure with those not directly involved in flying. He was not a particularly patient man, but he was a perfectionist. He expected everything to be in a tip-top condition for his 'boys' and did not always understand when things were not as he would have wanted them.

He understood the strain of flying, night after night, over enemy territory, never knowing whether the flight would end over the target or perhaps in the sea on the way home. The dangers experienced by the aircrews were real to him because he, too, experienced them. He knew the awful sick feeling while waiting for take-off; he understood the fear they felt when being fired at from the ground or from enemy fighters; he had felt the same relief that they felt when the raid was over and they were once more back on friendly soil with another night of hell behind them. He went to sleep after an operation, as they did, with the sound of the engines still in his ears, and his sleep, like theirs, was disturbed by the horrors he had witnessed night after night as he had seen his friends blown out of the sky.

Anyone not able to face up to this lifestyle was regarded as having a lack of moral fibre, a punishable offence according to the RAF. The ground staff did not have to suffer the same kind of stress as the aircrews and, as a pilot, Guy did not understand their problems and had very little empathy with them. Later on he came to appreciate the wonderful work performed by these men, often in difficult and uncomfortable conditions, and he realized that, without them, his work and that of others like him would not be possible. Unfortunately, during his time with 106 Squadron this realization had not yet dawned and he was never to have the close relationship with the ground crews that he enjoyed with the aircrews.

Off duty Guy was still a dedicated party-goer and liked nothing more than being able to let his hair down with his crews. He enjoyed having like-minded men around him. In the midst of a raid over enemy territory it was

vital to know that each crew member could be relied upon
to react instinctively to the actions of the others and this
kind of rapport had its foundations in their off-duty
behaviour.

Guy was usually accompanied to these social occasions
by Nigger who was, by now, quite a hardened drinker.
Woe betide anyone who let his arm hang over the side of
a chair whilst holding a pint pot. Nigger would have his
nose in the glass in a flash and the contents would be
gone. He was, however, a friendly dog and liked by most
of the squadron. He even had an Iron Cross, made
specially for him, which he wore attached to his collar.
Guy sometimes took his little friend on flights with him.
Nigger would curl up on the floor and go to sleep, quite
unconcerned about the noise and action which surrounded him. Man and dog were devoted to each other.

Guy's own friends were men similar to himself, extro-
vert party-goers: people like Robbo and Bill Whamond,
Dave Shannon, who came from Australia, and Guy's
particular friend, Hoppy Hopgood. But he had to be
especially careful not to show any favouritism to his own
circle of friends. It could sometimes be a lonely job, that
of Squadron Commander.

Whenever a 48 hour leave came along it was nice for
him to be able to get away from the worry of his job and
relax with his family. Sometimes this meant a trip to
London to be with Eve, who had left her job with the Red
Cross in Cardiff and was now working in a camouflage
netting factory in Victoria. She had moved into a flat in
Aberdeen Place, St. John's Wood, which she shared with
a friend. As time went on these visits became more
stressful than restful. The couple had begun to argue a lot
and there was usually an atmosphere whenever they
spent any time together. They could never agree on what
to do when Guy was on leave in London. He wanted to
go out, to the pub, to a party, to the theatre, anywhere
where there were bright lights, lots of people and some

20. The Startled Saint public house in West Malling, Kent. Built on the edge of the airfield it was the "local" used by 29 Squadron. (*via Robin Brooks*)

21. 29 Squadron, West Malling, late 1941. Officer Commanding, Wing Commander Colbeck-Welch seated centre with his Flight Commanders Guy Gibson (left) and Bob Braham. (*via Chaz Bowyer*)

22. Guy with his drinking partner, Nigger. (*Janet de Gaynesford*)

23. Guy in thoughtful mood, prior to take-off. (*Imperial War Museum*)

24. Guy (right) with his wireless operator, Pilot Officer R.E.G. Hutchison. (*Imperial War Museum*)

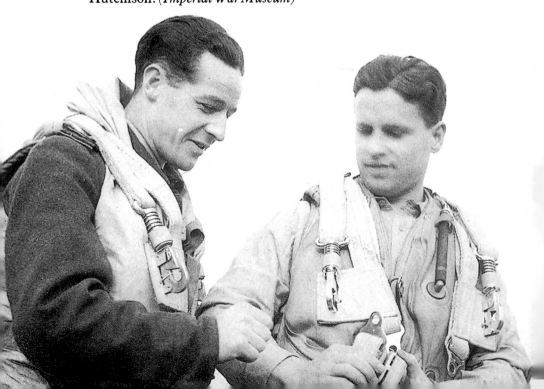

25. W/Cdr Gus Walker and crew, 50 Squadron, Hampden X/VN. Far right, Sgt R.A.D. Trevor-Roper (Air Gunner), Later F/Lt, DFC, DFM, Gibson's rear gunner on the Dams raid. He was killed on 31 March, 1944. *(via Chaz Bowyer)*

26. Guy Gibson, in the centre, in front of Lancaster 1, ED593, "Admiral Prune 11", at RAF Syerston with, left, "B" flight commander, John Searby and, right, "A" flight commander Peter Ward-Hunt. *(RAF Museum)*

27 RAF Coningsby, 1 June, 1942. Guy and 106 Squadron crews after 1000 bomber raid on Cologne. (*Brian Robinson*)

28. Eve Gibson at her home in St. John's Wood, with a photo of her husband. (*Derrick Warren*)

29. The RAF wings brooch sent by Guy to his cousin, Janet, for her ninth birthday, one week before the Dams raid. (*Ian Ottaway*)

30. Guy and his crew climbing aboard their Lancaster before leaving RAF Scampton to bomb the Mohne Dam. Left to right, Trevor Roper, Pulford, Deering, Spafford, Hutchison, Gibson and Taerum. (*Imperial War Museum*)

31. Corporal Karl Schutte, commander of the north tower flak gun on the Möhne Dam, who was credited with the shooting down of AJ-M, "Hoppy" Hopgood's aircraft. The gun, a 20mm Flak 38, shows a white band which signifies a "kill". 23 year old Cpl Schutte is wearing the Iron Cross, second class, which he was awarded a week after the raid. (*Helmut Euler*)

32. Guy saluting the crowds during a procession for Maidstone Wings Week in June, 1943, accompanied by International Scout Commissioner Glad Bincham, seated far left. (*1st Tovil Scouts: Robin Brooks*)

33. H.M. The King meeting the ground crews of 617 Squadron. Second from right is the Squadron Armament Officer, Harry "Doc" Watson. (*Imperial War Museum*)

34. Guy talking to Roy Chadwick, designer of the Avro Lancaster, at Buckingham Palace. (*St. Edward's School Archives*)

35. Guy and Eve Gibson after the investiture at Buckingham Palace on 22 June, 1943. (*Sport and General Press Agency: St. Edward's School Archives*)

36. Guy signing his name across the breach in the Mohne Dam during a party held in honour of 617 Squadron on the evening of 22 June, 1943. (*RAF Museum*)

action. He needed this sort of atmosphere in which to unwind from the responsibility of the Squadron and all the men in it. Although it was a job that he wanted and executed in a very competent way it was a formidable responsibility for a man of only 23 and these short periods of leave were the only times that he could allow himself some relaxation. Eve, unfortunately, preferred to stay at home. Much later, after the war, she began to realize just how much stress Guy had suffered and why, when he was not flying, he drank so much.

When he did not go down to London to spend time with Eve, Guy visited his aunt and uncle at the Red House in Wales, much to the delight of Janet who was, by now, eight years old.

One evening Guy had arrived and was having dinner with her parents. Because of the bombing, Janet's bed had been moved to a downstairs room and it was in front of her window that Guy had parked his car. She was hanging out of the window when Guy came out to his car to fetch something. Seeing that she was not in bed, Guy came over to the window to talk to her. She was wearing a flowered nightdress but it was a warm night and Guy lifted her through the window and sat her in his car saying, 'Let's you and me run away together.' She was delighted and replied 'Oh, lovely. Can Nanny come too?' Guy thought this was very funny and said that it was not quite what he had in mind. He did, however, drive her down to the gates and back and then tucked her up in bed again before returning to the dining room to join her parents.

At the end of the first week in August, 1942, Guy was once again on 'gardening' trips to the Baltic. In atrocious weather, rain, mist and low cloud two trips were made on the 8th and 10th and both were successful in spite of the conditions under which they were made. On the outward leg on the 10th, whilst flying over Denmark, Guy spotted a Bf110 and, alerting the gunners, immediately

85

gave chase but was unable to take any action and the German managed to get away.

Guy's 24th birthday was on 12 August and he celebrated with a trip to Mainz. Eight aircraft out of a total of 150 were provided by 106 Squadron. The raid was very successful with a large area of the town destroyed and all but one of the 106 Squadron aircraft returned safely.

At the end of August Guy made his final raid of the month when he flew to Gdynia with a load of six 1000lb bombs. The target was the aircraft carrier *Graf Zeppelin* which was under construction, but this was not seen by the crew and they attacked the *Gneisenau* instead. The bomb aimer that night was Squadron Leader Richardson, a First World War veteran. The defences were fierce and the bomb aimer was anxious to place his bombs spot on the target. Consequently, Guy had to make 12 runs at the target before the Squadron Leader was satisfied. Even after taking all this care, the bombs did not reach the mark, missing the target by about 100 yards. Then came the long journey home with the danger of the defences over enemy territory and the rapidly approaching daylight.

The aircraft that Guy flew for this raid was W4118 'Y'. This was the aircraft that he had named *Admiral Prune*. The admiral idea had come, of course, from his days on 83 Squadron when the Hampdens had been so named. The most likely reason that he chose 'Prune' was after the fictional character, Pilot Officer Prune who appeared in the training manual, *Tee Emm*, and was everything an RAF officer should not be. This was, perhaps, Guy's way of laughing at himself, since he always regarded himself as an average pilot.

During the month of August 106 Squadron had carried out exactly 100 sorties over 15 nights and had dropped a total of 323 tons of bombs. This figure included 94 mines and the total was a new record.

On 1 September the target was Saarbrücken and the

load for this flight was one 8000lb bomb. This was the first time that Guy had flown in behind the Pathfinders. Unfortunately, that evening, although they marked the target well, they had found the wrong town and Saarbrücken was saved for another night at the expense of the little town of Saarlouis. Guy's navigator on this trip, Frank 'Junior' Ruskell, recalls how, on the following day, he pored over the map with a sinking heart, trying to fit the photo they had taken of Saarlouis on to the shape of Saarbrucken!

On 3 September the war entered its fourth year. In his logbook Guy decided to summarize his operational flying during the three previous years. He began with bomber flights of which he noted there had been six daylight and 50 night sorties, making a total of 332.45 hours. This in itself was a formidable total. When added to the 99 fighter sorties that he recorded on the following page the total became quite incredible.

On 1 October Guy made the 30-minute flight from Coningsby to Syerston when 106 Squadron moved to this Nottinghamshire airfield, after it was decided to lay concrete runways at Coningsby. This was a popular move and everyone was delighted to be serving under the Station Commander, Group Captain Gus Walker, who was a highly respected officer.

Syerston was also the home of 61 Squadron. When, one day, a WAAF intelligence officer from this Squadron arrived in the 106 Squadron offices with a message for Guy he assumed that she was the WAAF who had asked if she could have a flight in a Lancaster. Ignoring her protests, he rushed her out to the dispersal and, discovering that the pilot he had in mind to take her on a trip had already left, he took her over to another crew who were themselves having one of their first flights in a Lancaster. The poor pilot was new to the Squadron and not yet fully trained, the last thing he needed at that stage was a passenger. Guy, however, had said that the WAAF could have a flight and he was not going to go back on his word. It was just unfortunate that he had picked the wrong one and had not listened to her protests. The poor girl came back describing the flight as the most horrific of her career.

On 17 October No. 5 Group mounted a huge daylight attack on the Schneider armament works at Le Creusot in occupied France. The secondary target was the Montchanin transformer station which Guy, flying *Admiral Prune*, attacked along with Hoppy Hopgood. The attack was made from less than five hundred feet and was a great success, although a lot of damage was done to the aircraft.

Shortly afterwards the focus of the bombing was switched to Italian targets, as what was known as the Italian season began on the same night as the Battle of El Alamein.

Italy was usually popular with the crews as the flak was very light. Italian targets were almost regarded as a rest, for the Italians did not seem to be either willing or able to defend themselves to any great degree. Guy, perhaps, summed up the feeling in *Enemy Coast Ahead* when he said: 'Why bomb the Italian fleet the whole time? It never put to sea anyway.'

However, bomb Italy they did and over the next month Guy made a total of five flights to Italy, attacking targets, including the Italian fleet, at Genoa, Milan and Turin. In his logbook he wrote about a daylight trip to Milan almost as if it were a holiday excursion when he said, 'A marvellous trip with most magnificent scenery over the Alps.'

During November 106 Squadron had a change of Flight Commander. John Searby, who was later to become an Air Commodore, DSO, DFC, arrived to take over 'B' Flight. His first meeting with Guy was not particularly pleasant. Guy was tired and had been on ops the previous night when some Squadron aircraft had failed to return. His greeting to the new Flight Commander was bad tempered, bordering on the downright rude. When they met later Guy managed to redeem himself somewhat and the two eventually understood each other and developed a mutual respect.

For Guy nothing was allowed to come between him and his purpose of attacking the enemy. He tackled this objective with as much single-minded determination as he had the task of joining the RAF five years before. No one was going to come in his way and if his methods were sometimes a little unorthodox, so be it. Eve Gibson was to say after the war that she felt she had always come second to whichever aeroplane Guy happened to be flying at the time and that, although they were married for nearly four years, she never felt that she really knew him as he was so wrapped up in his work.

One thing was certain. In spite of his own assessment of himself as being an average pilot, by this stage of his career he was regarded by others as being an excellent pilot and an outstanding leader. This was reflected on 10 November when he was awarded the DSO as a result of the raids on Le Creusot and various Italian targets.

A week later, on 18 November, after a raid on the Fiat works at Turin, Guy was forced to land at Middle Wallop on his return, because of bad weather at the home base. Here he and the other crews were given lavish hospitality. When the weather at Syerston remained bad they stayed for a second night at Middle Wallop. Instead of enjoying the brief respite, Guy's mood became gloomy as he witnessed the fighter pilots from this station relaxing with very little to do. He resented the fact that his crews were facing danger and perhaps death nearly every night whilst the fighter crews lived in comparative comfort and, as there had not been very many enemy aircraft around at that time, were doing very little flying. Having served on a fighter squadron, he of all people should have understood the situation. However, so complete was his dedication to his bomber crews that his mind was closed to everything except their work and their welfare.

This dedication became something of a problem when Guy went on leave. He often found that he could not close his mind to what was happening on the Squadron and, more than once, cancelled his leave and returned to base. Sometimes his anxiety to return to his Squadron was caused by a blazing row with Eve. Whatever the reason the plans made by the two Flight Commanders were often disrupted by Guy's early return and they found that a great degree of patience was needed at times such as these. Guy did not tell anyone about his personal problems and the Flight Commanders were at a loss to know the cause of this erratic behaviour.

The Italian season of 1942 ended, for Guy at least, on 28 November when he took off at 19.00 hours with the No. 5 Group flak liaison officer as a passenger. They returned at 03.00 hours the next morning having again attacked Turin. Guy described the raid in his logbook as having been a 'grand prang'. They bombed from 8000 feet using one 8000lb bomb. After this had been dropped Guy flew backwards and forwards over the target taking a movie film of the damage which covered the centre of the town.

During November, 1942, 106 Squadron operated throughout the month without any loss of aircraft. This was the first month since January, 1941, that there had been no losses on the Squadron, an excellent record that was, no doubt, due in some way to the fact that the Italian targets they had been bombing were not as heavily defended as their German counterparts.

Unfortunately during December, when the weather was dreadful and flying was only possible on six nights during the entire month, three aircraft were lost.

The New Year of 1943 brought a visitor to 106 Squadron when, on 10 January, Major Richard Dimbleby, the BBC war correspondent, arrived to spend a few days, waiting for the special job to which he had been assigned. Usually Guy hated this type of visit and resented the time he had to spend showing the visitor around. On this occasion, however, he was pleased to have Major Dimbleby with the Squadron. This change of heart by Guy was probably due to the Major's willingness to fit in with the Squadron and also to his total lack of self-importance.

Leaving his visitor at Syerston, Guy flew off the following day to bomb the city of Essen, always regarded as a hot target by bomber crews. The job was completed with bombs dropped on the Pathfinders' flares, but the results were difficult to judge as the target was covered with cloud. In spite of fierce opposition all the Squadron's aircraft returned safely. Guy and his crew were embarrassed to learn on their return that they had inadvertently left the R/T on transmit!

The sixteenth of January was the date of the special job for which Richard Dimbleby had been sent to Syerston. The target was Berlin and he flew, as a passenger, in Guy's aircraft. This was a big raid. 106 Squadron sent 13 aircraft out of the total of 201 and there was only one loss overall in spite of the fierce defences. The weather over the target did not live up to the forecaster's expectations and there was considerable cloud covering the city. The outward route took the aircraft over the Baltic, and on the way there the heating went off in the mid-upper gunner's suit. The wireless operator, Pilot Office Hutchison, went to fix it and, having done so, collapsed on the floor because of lack of oxygen. He was, in turn, rescued by the navigator, Flying Officer Ruskell, who was away from his post for so long that the turning point at Stettin was missed. This problem was soon rectified, however, and they pressed on to Berlin. Three runs in all were made over the target before the bomb aimer was satisfied and released the 8000lb bomb from a height of 18,000 feet. this meant that the aircraft was in the flak over Berlin for about half an hour and it was a frightening experience, especially for Richard Dimbleby who, at this point, became sick.

After a flight totalling eight hours and 40 minutes the

aircraft landed back at Syerston, having had to hold over the aerodrome for an hour and twenty minutes.

The following day Richard Dimbleby made a broadcast about his experiences which was tannoyed all over RAF Syerston. In it he described the trip as a 'pretty hair-raising experience' and said that he was glad when it was over, although he would not have missed it for the world.

He described how the crews flew out, night after night, to some of the hottest targets in Germany and emphasized that the work they did was hard, tiring and dangerous. He went on to explain the sensation of enemy fire bursting all around the aircraft and how the crew handled it, with the words, 'Sometimes it closes in on you and the mid or tail gunner will call up calmly and report its position to the captain so that he can dodge it. We dodged it last night particularly over Berlin. Literally jumped over it and nipped around, with the Wing Commander sitting up in his seat as cool as a cucumber, pushing and pulling his great bomber about as though it were a toy.'

Major Dimbleby found it a fascinating thought that somewhere, a few thousand feet below their aircraft, Hitler, Himmler, Göring or Goebbels might be cowering in a shelter, trying to protect themselves from the huge bomb that his aircraft had dropped.

There is a slight discrepancy in the three different accounts of the flight about the names of the crew that night. Guy has listed them in his logbook as Flying Officer Ruskell, Flight Lieutenant Oliver, Pilot Officer Hutchison, Flying Officer Wickins, Sergeant McGregor and a naval officer, Sub Lieutenant Muttrie. Frank Ruskell remembers a Rhodesian called Ian McNair as being the bomb aimer. Richard Dimbleby lists the crew in the final remarks of his talk as follows:- 'Johnny (Wickins) from the tail turret, Brian (Oliver) who used to be a policeman, from the mid-upper, Hutch, the radio operator, Junior, the navigator, by far the youngest of us all and then the Scotch co-pilot, a quiet calm sergeant and last the short, sturdy Wingco, who's flown in every major air raid of this war and has been a night fighter pilot in between times. They were the crew. Six brave, cool and exceedingly skilful men. Perhaps I am shooting a line for them but I think that somebody ought to. They and their magnificent Lancasters and all the others like them are taking the war right into Germany.'

Guy's Squadron was not only taking the war right into Germany, they were also taking it to occupied France and to Italy as well. Their next operation after the Berlin raid was to Milan on St Valentine's Day, 1943. His was one of 11 aircraft which the Squadron sent on this, most successful, raid. Ten 106 Squadron aircraft bombed accurately and brought back six aiming point photographs, which the AOC No. 5 Group pointed out in a letter of congratulation, was a record. Guy stayed over the target for longer than most and for 20 minutes took a movie film of the raid.

A trip to Nuremberg followed, during which the Pathfinders arrived late and the attacking force of 350 aircraft were forced to circle the target whilst waiting for them.

Cologne was the target for Guy's penultimate operation with 106 Squadron. It took place the night after the Nuremberg raid and was his 70th bombing mission. Although the target was heavily defended, the bombing appeared to be accurate and Guy described the raid as a 'wizard prang'.

Guy's final trip with the Squadron came on 11 March, 1943. The target was Stuttgart and on this trip he was taking a pilot new to the Squadron, a Canadian Flying Officer named Walter Thompson, who had only arrived that afternoon.

The flight was beset with problems and, when the port outer engine died on the outward journey, Guy had to decide whether or not to abandon the operation. He was due to go on leave and had no desire to postpone his trip to Cornwall, so decided to press on with three engines at a low level. This was done, but involved more danger, as he was below the main force of aircraft and stood a chance of being hit by one of their bombs. The explosions from these bombs also caused huge updraughts which threw Guy's aircraft around alarmingly. However, the trip was successfully completed and he returned to Syerston to say farewell to his Squadron.

Before Guy had the chance to depart on his short break his leave was cancelled and he was posted to Headquarters No. 5 Group on 15 March, handing over command to 'B' Flight commander, John Searby. A farewell party was quickly arranged during which Guy made what he described as a 'rotten speech' before getting down to the serious business of drinking!

So ended his first command. He had been with the Squadron for 11 months and had taken part in all the major raids the Squadron had mounted. Under his leadership 106 Squadron had risen to the number one position in the whole of No. 5 Group and for his work Guy was awarded on 25 March a bar to his DSO. The citation for the award paid tribute to his work saying:-

'This officer has an outstanding operational record, having completed 172 sorties. He has always displayed the greatest keenness and, within the past two months, has taken part in six attacks against well defended targets, including Berlin.

'In March, 1943, he captained an aircraft detailed to attack Stuttgart. On the outward flight engine trouble developed but he flew on to his objective and bombed it from a low level.

'This is typical of his outstanding determination to make every sortie a success.

'By his skilled leadership and contempt for danger he has set an example which has inspired the squadron he commands.'

Although he was disliked by some, his skills as a pilot and as a leader were acknowledged by all. The men respected him for never expecting them to attempt anything he would not do himself and he kept their good opinion by including himself, whenever possible, on the crew list for the more dangerous operations.

Guy's own crew were happy to fly anywhere with him and had complete confidence in his ability to get them safely to the target and back home again.

When on the ground he found his desk job more taxing than flying, but he tackled it with determination. He did have a compassionate streak which he was sometimes loath to show, but it was, nonetheless, there and extended not only to his men but, on occasions, to their families as well.

When an aircraft was missing or had crashed it was Guy's task to inform the next of kin of the crew. Many letters had to be written during Guy's stay with 106 Squadron and he always tried to make them personal notes rather than the standard notice so often sent to grieving families. This can, perhaps, be best illustrated by the letter Guy wrote to the mother of Flight Lieutenant Gray Healey when he went missing after a flight on 13 January, 1943.

Although the first part of the letter has been typewritten it does contain some personal remarks. Before giving the usual details about information coming from the International Red Cross Committee, Guy says that 'Everyone on the Squadron and the Station feel deeply for you and your husband on this news, and we all would like you to know that we thought he was the best ever.' He finishes the letter in his own handwriting by saying: 'Please accept my heartfelt sympathy and please be brave until you hear more news. I know how hard it is and you can rest assured that the boys and I will hit those Huns even harder for doing this to you.'

When a freshman crew joined the Squadron Guy always tried to ease them in gently by sending them for their first few trips to easy targets or to lay mines. Although this did, of course, make sound sense to the Squadron, it also gave the new Squadron members a chance to find their feet and was much appreciated by them.

Guy always tried to make his boys welcome and Flying Officer Walter Thompson, who accompanied him to Stuttgart on his last operation with the Squadron, remembers him as being one of the friendliest Wing Commanders he had ever met. He took the trouble to introduce the young Flying Officer to other members of the Squadron. Much later Walter Thompson was to write of him that he 'had a faint air of the First World War about him; because there was a war on was no reason for lapses of courtesy, warmth and modest behaviour.'*

* *Lancaster to Berlin* by Walter Thompson, DFC and bar. (Published by Goodall Publications Ltd 1985)

Chapter 7

DAMBUSTER

When Guy's leave was cancelled he was dismayed to discover that he had been posted to HQ No. 5 Group. He had been hoping that he would be given duties linked with operations during the time he was to be rested from operational flying. It now seemed that this would be unlikely. This dismay was, however, short-lived as he was soon summoned to the office of Air Vice-Marshal the Hon Ralph Cochrane, AOC No. 5 Group, who asked him if he would be prepared to do one more trip. He, of course, agreed but soon began to wonder if he hadn't been a little hasty in his agreement. Although he was not told what the target would be he began working things out in his own mind from the scant information available and decided that he had probably just volunteered to attack the *Tirpitz*, a task not relished by anyone.

Guy was surprised to learn that he would not take command of an existing squadron but would be instrumental in forming a new one, specifically for the purpose of carrying out this one raid. This was more like it; more than even he had dared to hope. At least it showed that his hard work and excellent results with 106 Squadron had been noticed.

He was told that he would have complete control over the formation of the squadron and that he had the authority to request anything or anyone that he needed. Of the actual raid he was told nothing, only that he would need crews able to fly at low level over water.

His first task was to draw up a list of men who he thought would be suitable. The selection of the pilots was relatively easy and most were men known personally to Guy. Some were picked for their expertise and daring; others for their consistency and reliability. Guy had, at this stage in his career, become quite adept at picking the right man for the right job. He was single-minded enough about his own career to recognize the same quality in others and he knew he would need men who would give their all to the task, whatever it might prove to be. With the selection of the other crew members Guy was given some help. Although most had a lot of experience this was not true of all the crews and some were not even close to completing their first tour.

The squadron was to be based at RAF Scampton, which had been home to Guy during his days with 83 Squadron, and was under the command of Group Captain J. Whiteworth. The new squadron, which initially was known as Squadron X, was to share the station with 57 Squadron. At the end of March Squadron X was given its proper designation and 617 Squadron was born.

The aircraft which would be used for this special task were Avro Lancasters which had to be quite extensively adapted to accommodate the bomb which had been designed specifically for the raid.

As the crews began arriving at Scampton they found that conditions were somewhat primitive. 49 Squadron, who had previously been at Scampton, had moved out because the airfield was about to be equipped with concrete runways and they had taken almost everything with them. There were no chairs or tables and not enough beds for the hundreds of men that make up a squadron. At first everything had to be scrounged or borrowed and the men themselves made a game of spotting and 'requisitioning' necessary items. The other squadron on the station had to look out for its own equipment. Left alone for even a few minutes it might easily disappear.

The hand-picked crew members began arriving at Scampton towards the end of March and all were curious as to why they were there. Some arrived as part of a complete crew. Others found that they had been separated from their normal crews for various reasons, but they soon found themselves new crew members and all settled in quite quickly in spite of the problems of forming a new squadron in such a hurry.

Guy picked for his two Flight Commanders Squadron Leader H. M. Young, DFC and Squadron Leader H. E. Maudslay, DFC. Squadron Leader Young was a former Oxford rowing blue and had already completed two tours. He came from 57 Squadron. Twice he had had to ditch into the sea and this experience led to him being given the nickname of Dinghy. Squadron Leader Maudslay was an old Etonian and arrived at the new squadron from 50 Squadron.

He was also pleased to have with him three pilots from 106 Squadron, Burpee, Shannon and, of course, his old friend Hoppy Hopgood. Guy's own wireless operator, Flight Lieutenant Hutchison from 106 Squadron, rejoined him shortly after his arrival at Scampton. The Australian low-flying expert, Micky Martin, was also included, as was the tall blond American, Joe McCarthy. Other crews came from Australia, New Zealand and Canada.

From the start it became clear that many questions would be asked about the formation of this new squadron and that no answers would be given until the mission for which they had been formed had taken place. Guy, always a strict disciplinarian, now issued dire threats to anyone who spoke out of turn or breached any security regulations. He stressed how important it was to keep silent about what was happening at Scampton and, in truth, there was very little that could be said at that stage anyway. At the start even he was unaware of the target.

This omission was quickly rectified after Guy went down to Surrey to meet the man who would be providing the crews with the special weapon needed for this raid, Barnes Wallis.

Barnes Wallis had been expecting to talk completely freely with the Wing Commander chosen to undertake this project and was amazed when he discovered that Guy had not been informed of the target. Guy's lack of information made it more difficult for the scientist to discuss the finer points of his invention, but he did show Guy a film of the trials that had already been carried out. For the first time Guy saw a film of the amazing weapon that his squadron would use: the bouncing bomb.

Shortly after his first meeting with Wallis, Guy was informed by AVM Cochrane at No. 5 Group HQ in Grantham that the target would be the dams of the Ruhr, at the heart of Germany's industrial area.

Returning to visit Barnes Wallis at his office in Weybridge, Surrey, Guy was now able to discuss the project from an informed viewpoint and pilot and inventor set about the task of ironing out the difficulties that they would each, no doubt, encounter.

Back at Scampton the Squadron was training hard. Guy was still the only one to know the target, but he told the others enough for them to guess that the raid would be made over water and at a low level. Speculation was rife, the most popular view being that the target was either the *Tirpitz* or, perhaps, U-boat pens.

Whenever he was at Scampton Guy trained just as hard as the others, but much of his time was spent with administration work, planning the most daring raid yet to be undertaken by the RAF. His own crew found that they were flying every evening because it was generally the only time available to Guy for training. They decided that they didn't really mind as it kept them off the 'booze'.

He was also involved with the trials still being carried out on the bomb which was code-named Upkeep. Security was so tight that whenever Guy went down to visit Barnes Wallis he used different modes of transport and different routes so that no one would know where he had been. Although the bomb worked in theory and small practice bombs had worked in reality, there were still a lot of tests to be carried out before Barnes Wallis was satisfied that it would work properly on the day. Many test drops were made at Chesil Beach in Dorset and at Reculver Bay in Kent. Whenever it was possible Guy attended these trials and, at first, witnessed the disappointing results, as the casings of the bombs broke up as they hit the water.

Barnes Wallis had asked Guy if it was possible for the pilots to fly the aircraft at a height of 150 feet and this they managed to do. However, when it became obvious that the casing was breaking each time because the bomb was being dropped from too great a height he revised his calculations and Guy was requested to fly at a height of 60 feet. Guy took this news back to his Squadron and they set about trying to devise a way of accurately measuring their height. The crews found that, during the day, this request was not too difficult to fulfil but at night, with the ground almost entirely obscured from view, it was practically impossible. Micky Martin was the expert on low flying, but even he did not have the answer. Aircraft were landing back at Scampton after low flying trials with bits of tree branches and leaves stuck in their undercarriages. The problem was even worse when flying over water as there was no way of judging the height at all, but the problem was finally resolved by a man from the Ministry of Aircraft Production.

His solution was quite simple. He suggested that two lamps be fitted to the underside of the aircraft. If these were placed at the correct angle their beams would converge at the exact height that Barnes Wallis required. Hurriedly the lamps were fitted to an aeroplane and it was sent off on a test flight. It worked and the problem had been solved.

For most of the crews training took place during the day as well as in the evening and there arose the problem of simulating moonlight whilst flying in daylight. Someone suggested using sunglasses but that did not work as it was almost impossible to see the instruments whilst wearing them. Then it was discovered that there was a system of simulating moonlight by painting the screens blue and wearing yellow goggles. Once again an aircraft was modified in this way and a successful test was carried out.

There remained a problem with navigation. Since the aircraft would be flying really low they would appear to be moving faster across the ground below than if they were at a higher altitude. This meant that they would need large-scale maps and there arose the problem of how to cope with many maps during the flight without getting them all in a muddle. For some the answer was to stick them all together and then roll them. In this way the section already used could be wound up, leaving exposed the part currently being used.

A similar simple solution was found to the problem of a suitable bomb sight. Not only did the aircraft have to be flown at a specific height but the bomb had to be dropped at an exact distance from the target. A bomb sight was made which meant that this was possible. It was a V-shaped device with pins on each of the open ends. When these were lined up with the towers on the dams the aircraft was the exact distance away from the target for the bomb to be dropped. Although this was a very simple device it did not suit all the bomb aimers in the Squadron and some of them made their own arrangements by drawing parallel lines on the clear panel in the nose of the aircraft.

While all these problems were being solved and the crews were perfecting their low-flying techniques at night, Guy was still very busy. The tests were still being carried out on the bomb and one day Guy took the Squadron bombing leader, an Australian Flight Lieutenant named Bob Hay, with him when he went to watch one of these tests in Kent. After it was over the two men climbed into their Magister to fly back to base. They had only been airborne for a few minutes when the engine cut out and Guy frantically searched for an empty field in which to land. This proved to be quite difficult as most of the available space had been made unserviceable by various devices such as poles and barbed wire in case of a German invasion. Eventually, however, he did manage to find a small piece of ground but the aeroplane crashed on landing. Luckily both Guy and Bob Hay were unhurt but were very amused when a man ran up to see if they were all right and, looking at them both, stated that he thought the RAF made people as young as they were fly too early.

As if a crash at this stage was not bad enough Guy had developed a carbuncle on the side of his face which was very painful. Using his oxygen mask made it even worse and he went to the doctor to see what could be done about it. The doctor said that he thought Guy had been working much too hard and that the carbuncle had appeared because he was run down. The solution was simple. He prescribed a complete rest for a couple of weeks. Guy could only laugh at this suggestion and put up with the pain and inconvenience.

Guy had very little relaxation at all during this period. Sometimes when time permitted he would go for long walks with Nigger. He had been given permission to use the grounds of a nearby country estate for these walks and sometimes he took Nigger out in a boat on the lake which formed part of the estate. He enjoyed this time spent away from everyone as it gave him time to think without being distracted by the pressures of life on the Squadron. As he had discovered with his last command, it was sometimes a lonely job being a squadron commander. Although he had friends on the Squadron, there was really no one to whom he could turn without being accused of favouritism. So be began to regard Nigger as his best friend and the quiet moments he spent in the countryside with his dog were very precious to him.

When he did allow himself a few hours for a party, he

always enjoyed himself, although, as Squadron Commander, he remained more sober than he had in the past. He liked nothing more than a riotous party but his work still came first; nothing was going to stop him from making the best possible job that he could of this assignment.

It has been said of Guy that he did not have anything to do with the NCOs on the Squadron. This was not true. He simply did not have much time or opportunity to mix with anyone. He had, however, discovered that two Squadron members were keen swimmers. These were the Canadian pilot Flight Sergeant Ken Brown and his English flight engineer, Sergeant Basil Feneron who, on the night of the raid, bombed the Sorpe dam. On a few occasions Guy accompanied them when they went into Lincoln to the swimming baths and was able to forget his responsibilities for an hour or two while they all messed about in the water. Guy was just as active in the horseplay as were the other two and on one occasion sneaked up behind Ken Brown, who was wearing a smart bathing robe that he had borrowed from Basil Feneron, and pushed him into the pool.

At the beginning of May Guy was dismayed to discover a serious breach in security. The armament officer, Pilot Officer H 'Doc' Watson, had spent three weeks at Manston in Kent during April in connection with the bombing trials. When he returned to Scampton, he told Guy that three days after his arrival at Manston he had been shown a file which contained diagrams, maps and other secret details connected with the forthcoming raid. Guy was furious when he realized that at the time Pilot Officer Watson had been given this information he knew more than either of the Flight Commanders did. In fact he knew more than Guy himself did at that stage. He was even more upset when he learned from Pilot Officer Watson that he was not alone when this information had been given to him and that an officer from 618 Squadron had also been shown the file. Guy immediately had a very serious talk with Pilot Officer Watson and stressed the need for complete security. He then wrote a strong letter to the senior staff officer at HQ No. 5 Group in Grantham, explaining what had happened and pointing out that, in his opinion, it was completely unnecessary for an armament officer to have any of this information. Air Vice-Marshal Cochrane, AOC No. 5 Group, agreed with Guy and the officer who had shown Pilot Officer Watson the file had it removed from his charge, and was severely reprimanded for putting the security of the entire operation in jeopardy.

The flying training continued during the first part of May without any mishaps. The only people who really felt they were suffering were the local farmers. A number of them considered that the Squadron's low-level flying was disturbing their animals and some complaints were received at Scampton. Nevertheless the low-level flying continued. Much of it was done over water at Uppingham Lake, Colchester Reservoir and the Derwent Dam.

Gradually the numerous problems were ironed out and there remained only the problem of the bomb itself. After a number of tests, these problems were also resolved and the actual bomb used on the raid was slightly different in appearance from the one first envisaged by Barnes Wallis. The outer casing, which had kept breaking, was removed and the finished bomb looked something like a large oil drum. Since it was of an unconventional shape and size it was not possible to carry it in the bomb bay and it had to be slung under the aircraft which had to be adapted. In addition to its size and shape, the bomb was also unique in that, to perform correctly, it needed to be spun backwards before being released. The equipment that was needed for this task had also to be housed in the adapted aircraft.

The date set for the raid on the dams was around 19 May, 1943. This depended on the level of the water in the reservoirs and photo-reconnaissance aircraft had been regularly sent out to photograph the dams in the weeks leading up to the raid. The crews were briefed to ascertain the water level and to note any changes being made at the dams, so ensuring that the Germans were not expecting an attack. There was a moment of concern when it was discovered that the Germans had placed some tall, pointed objects along the top of the Möhne dam, but these were later found to be ornamental conifers used to beautify rather than defend the structure.

Although the day was fast approaching when the raid would be carried out, the men of 57 Squadron were beginning to wonder if 617 Squadron would ever do anything. They had spent such a lot of time training while the other Squadron at Scampton had been making many operational flights that it was not surprising that they were teased as being armchair pilots. Very soon, however, that all changed.

Micky Martin, recalling the week before the raid, remembered how they all tried to fit in as much living as possible during that week. Although they had not been told what the target would be, they all knew that it was a very special raid and most believed that it would be so dangerous that the chances of returning were probably quite slim. In these circumstances it seemed a shame to leave anything undone and even more of a waste to leave any money unspent. Guy himself spent some money that week in buying a birthday present of a gold and enamel brooch for his young cousin Janet. He never forgot her at Christmas time or on her birthday and had no intentions of doing so now, just because he had only one week to go before the raid. Janet was thrilled to receive the gift, her first piece of real jewellery, for her ninth birthday.

Unlike his crews, Guy knew, rather than surmised, that the target would be a dangerous one. It was obvious that the dams were very important to the Germans and they would not let them be destroyed without a good fight.

Worse still for Guy was the fact that he would be leading the raid and would be the first to discover just how strong these defences were.

Even when he was given the date of the raid as the night of Sunday, 16 May Guy could not relax for a moment. There were still little last minute problems which occurred and he had to write out the operation order in great detail. This task was completed on 15 May, the day after the full dress rehearsal at Uppingham Lake when Guy was accompanied by the Station Commander, Group Captain Whitworth. It was a complete success.

Since it had been decided that Guy would co-ordinate the entire operation by radio, one of the first instances of using a 'Master bomber', certain code words were devised to simplify the procedure. Words such as 'Dinghy' and 'Nigger' would signify that the targets had been destroyed.

It was, perhaps, a horrible irony that the word 'Nigger' should have been chosen to mean the destruction of a target, for, on the night of 15 May as Guy was writing out his operation orders, his beloved dog Nigger was killed by a car outside the main gates at Scampton. Group Captain Whitworth brought Guy the awful news and told him that Nigger's body had been brought into the guard room.

It is not hard to imagine how Guy must have felt at that moment. Nigger had been his faithful companion since he first came to live with him as a puppy down in Kent. They had shared so much and, when times were hard for Guy, Nigger had always been there with a friendly greeting for his master. The dog's death was a devastating blow for Guy, and coming, as it did, the day before the most important mission he had ever flown, was a disaster. He was, however, a true professional in his work and was determined not to let this personal tragedy affect the raid. His time for grieving would have to wait until the raid had been satisfactorily carried out. Knowing that some of the crews might regard Nigger's death as a bad omen, Guy asked that they should not be told until after their return.

The next morning Guy arranged the burial of his dog. He did not want to do it himself but asked that it be carried out at midnight that night, which was the time he was due to be over the target. He spoke to a Flight Sergeant in the station workshop and asked him to build a coffin for Nigger but the man refused and a row ensued. Guy, perhaps understandably, completely lost his temper, but did not get the coffin for his dog. He left the details of the burial to Flight Sergeant Powell, 617's disciplinary NCO. The burial was carried out, exactly as he had requested and at midnight his little friend was laid to rest. Marked much later by a proper stone, the carefully tended little grave remains to this day on the grass outside the original 617 Squadron offices at RAF Scampton.

Sunday, 16 May was a hot day and the forecast for the raid remained good. During the day the crews were told what their targets would be and they spent some hours examining the models of the dams and fixing the details in their minds.

When the time came to leave there was great excitement and almost the entire station turned out to wave 617 on their way. As Guy was climbing into his Lancaster a photographer drove up to take a photo of the departing crew. Guy, in shirt-sleeves, stopped at the top of the ladder and turned. His crew, still on the ground, turned also and the photo was taken. Guy told the photographer that 'just in case' he had better send a copy to his wife and his crew laughed. As they disappeared into the aircraft, their laughter could still be heard. They obviously thought Guy's statement to be ridiculous. They would be coming back; there was no doubt about that in the minds of any of them.

Guy in his Lancaster, AJ-G, took off at 21.39 hours accompanied by Hoppy Hopgood in AJ-M and Micky

Martin in AJ-P. They were followed minutes later by six more aircraft, including those of the two Flight Commanders. These nine aircraft would make the attack on the main targets of the Möhne and Eder dams. Then came five more crews heading for the Sorpe dam. The remaining aircraft out of the total of 19 would be used wherever they were needed and could be contacted by radio to be given their orders.

Much has been written about the raid and its consequences. It was, of course, a great success, although in terms of crews lost it was an expensive operation. Of the 19 aircraft which left Scampton that May evening only 11 were to return. From the eight aircraft lost, only three men would survive.

The outward flight for Guy and his two companions was relatively peaceful, at least until they reached the Dutch coast. As they approached the Möhne dam they flew over the Rhine and down towards the Möhne Lake which was calm and still and looked like a mirror in the moonlight.

Guy made a dummy run over the dam and then came in to line up for his attack. The flak was quite heavy but the attack was successfully made and the aircraft was not damaged. The bomb dropped in the correct place and as it exploded a huge wall of water was thrown into the night air. It took several minutes for the spray to subside and when it did the dam was seen to be still intact.

Guy then called in Hoppy to make his run. As he approached the wall his aircraft was hit and his bomb was released a little too late. Instead of bouncing up to the dam wall and then sinking it dropped over the top of the dam and landed on a power station on the other side, exploding immediately. This explosion may have destroyed one of the flak guns. Hoppy called for the crew to bale out and tried to climb while they were doing so to give them a better chance of survival. It was no good. Only two members of the crew managed to bale out and live to tell the tale. A third left the aircraft, but did not survive the fall. Seconds later the aircraft crashed with a huge explosion and the subsequent fire burned for a long time, a constant reminder to the other crews of the dangers they were facing.

Guy, circling around and watching this, was helpless to do anything. He told his uncle and aunt later that when he saw his friend shot down something inside him snapped and all he could think of was to get whoever had been responsible for Hoppy's death.

As he called Micky Martin in to make the third attack, Guy decided to fly along with him in order to try to divert the flak from the attacking aircraft to his own. This worked and although Martin's aircraft was hit he was able to make a successful attack and, ultimately, return to England.

When Guy flew in alongside the other aircraft, the gunners in AJ-G fired furiously at the gun emplacements on the dam. In spite of their efforts the man credited with shooting down AJ-M was not killed. He was Corporal Karl Schutte, 23-year-old commander of the North Tower flak gun, who survived the attack to be decorated, a week later, with the Iron Cross, 2nd class.

It took two more bombs before the dam was finally breached by the one dropped from David Maltby's aircraft. As each aircraft made their bombing run Guy flew alongside diverting the flak. Then on they went to the Eder dam where Guy, once more, directed the attack. After it was hit by the third bomb, delivered by Les Knight and his crew, the Eder dam also collapsed with a huge hole across its middle. It had not been necessary to use diversionary tactics at this dam. There were no flak positions on its walls as there had been at the Möhne. The Eder dam was in a difficult position to reach at low level with a large aircraft and the Germans had obviously thought an attack to be impossible. They had not reckoned with the tenacity of the men of 617 Squadron.

The return journey was filled with a mixture of elation

and sadness. The task had been completed but at what cost. In a misspelt entry in his logbook Guy said simply of the raid, 'Led attack on Möhne an[d] Eder dams. Successful.'

Chapter 8

FOR VALOUR

At 07.25 on the morning of Monday, 17 May, 1943, a Spitfire XI, EN343, of 542 Squadron took off from the home of photographic reconnaissance, RAF Benson in Oxfordshire. Its pilot was Flying Officer F. G. Fray. Three hours and 35 minutes later he returned to Benson having taken what is probably one of the most famous photographs of the war, that of the breached Möhne dam. His film was rushed to the photographic interpretation unit at nearby RAF Medmenham and from there to No. 5 Group headquarters at Grantham. The RAF made good use of this photograph and of the earlier photographs taken by Flying Officer Fray when they produced leaflets describing the operation and dropped them over the occupied European countries. For his part in the operation Flying Officer Fray was awarded the DFC.

On 18 May the men of 617 Squadron were given special leave; three days for the ground crews and seven days for the aircrew. For Guy, however, the work was not yet complete. For three days he sat in his office, overlooking the grave of his beloved friend, Nigger, and wrote letters to the families of those who had not returned. Each letter contained something different, something personal, and by the time he had completed the 56 letters he was physically and emotionally exhausted. Although he kept his feelings tightly under control, the loss of so many men affected him deeply. These were the boys with whom he had flown. They had lived side by side for the past two months, sharing a joke or the odd drink in the Mess and now they were gone. He knew it was not his fault and that an operation like this was bound to produce heavy casualties, but, nonetheless, they were his men and he felt responsible for them. The last thing he could do for them was to inform their families in a personal, sensitive way.

Eve Gibson thought that her husband had been grounded. That is what he had told her and she had no reason to believe anything different. Since she lived in London she had no way of knowing what Guy was doing on a day-to-day basis. She was, therefore, amazed when a friend told her what she had just heard on the wireless about the raid on the Ruhr dams.

Soon she was able to see for herself the reports that began appearing in the newspapers. Headlines such as 'DAMS WERE BURST BY ONLY NINETEEN LANCAS-TERS', '60 MILES OF FLOOD IN RUHR VALLEY' and 'LANCASTER ACE SMASHED HITLER'S RUHR DAMS' were commonplace in the first few days after the raid. In a few more days she herself would be interviewed by newspaper reporters and would coyly tell them, 'I thought my husband was pen-pushing. He never talks about his work.'

Back at No. 5 Group headquarters telegrams were coming in from, among others, Fighter Command, Coastal Command and the Secretary of State for Air, Sir Archibald Sinclair.

Sir Archibald said in a lengthy message that 'The thorough tactical planning, the energy and drive behind the special preparation and, finally, the determined execution of this operation have combined to deal a grievous blow to the enemy and are worthy of the highest praise.'

In his very brief message AOC-in-C Coastal Command, Sir John Slessor, said 'Well done 5 Group and Scampton. A magnificent night's work.'

The AOC-in-C Fighter Command, Sir Trafford Leigh-Mallory, was more effusive in his praise: 'Heartiest congratulations from all in Fighter Command on your magnificent exploit in wrecking the Möhne and Eder dams. Probably the greatest and most far-reaching destruction yet wreaked on Germany in a single night.'

The Germans themselves had to admit that the raid had caused a considerable amount of damage. It took 5000 men four-and-a-half months to repair the damage to the Möhne and Eder dams and the effects of the damage to the latter were still being felt as late as 1988 when it was discovered that the dam had moved several centimetres. In 1991 the site of the breach was, once again, being repaired.

There were other messages of praise, official and otherwise, not only for the Squadron but for the many other people involved in the entire operation. Barnes Wallis received a letter from Guy telling him how honoured he and his pilots were to have been part of the great experiment. He also said that Barnes Wallis had earned the thanks of the civilized world and went on to suggest that a holiday would be in order.

Guy himself was, by now, ready for a short break. Having completed his immediate post-raid duties, he went, with Eve, to spend a long weekend with his in-laws in Penarth.

Whilst visiting a club in Cardiff on 22 May Guy ran into another old boy of St Edward's School, Surgeon-Captain Stewart Goss, RN. Captain Goss was so impressed with Guy that on 24 May he wrote to the secretary of the St Edward's School society and gave his impressions of the meeting and his permission to quote from his letter in the *School Chronicle*, should he so desire. He said he had never met, in all his years of service, a more modest, charming, unspoilt and gallant lad but that it was only what he expected of an old boy of St Edward's.

The morning after Guy's meeting with Captain Goss he received a telephone call, at his in-laws' house, from Sir Arthur Harris informing him that he had been awarded the Victoria Cross. After replacing the receiver he stood in silence for a few moments, taking in the news. He was, of course, delighted, but could not help thinking of all the men lost on the raid and told Eve that it seemed unfair somehow. Later on that afternoon Guy telephoned his aunt and uncle and told them, rather apologetically, 'I'm afraid they've given me the Victoria Cross.'

Many more letters of praise flooded in, although not all of them came directly to Guy. The Rev Kendall, Warden of St Edward's School, received many letters of congratulation from old boys and their relatives and friends. One letter informed Warden Kendall 'You will be doubly interested to know that my David was on the raid and that he has been given the DSO,' and was signed Ettrick Maltby. All the correspondents were extremely proud that one of their own should have been so honoured.

Warden Kendall wrote, offering his own good wishes to Guy on the success of the raid and received a reply, dated 25 May, in which Guy added 'P.S. Was awarded VC yesterday.' Guy wrote again on 30 May in reply to the Warden's letter of congratulation upon the award of his VC. He began by saying that he thought that the stuff which had appeared in the papers was 'pretty good tripe' and closed with 'All the "old boys" have done wonderfully, and it is to those who have fallen, I think, that we ought to raise our glasses.'

At the end of May King George VI and Queen Elizabeth began a 500-mile, two-day tour of seven RAF stations and two US Army Air Corps bases. During a visit to one of the latter they had been shown a B17 Flying Fortress, the Memphis Belle which, with its crew, had just completed its 25th daylight raid. Twenty-five missions was a record for the Americans and the crew, shortly after meeting the Royal visitors, were sent home as heroes. A film, directed by William Wyler, was made about the Memphis Belle and her crew.

On 27 May the Royal couple made a lunchtime visit to

Scampton and met the men of 617 Squadron who were, by this time, being referred to as 'dambusters'. Guy was, of course, introduced to them both and he accompanied the King on his tour of inspection. Each crew was lined up in a separate group and the royal visitors made their way down the lines, meeting the men who had survived the raid. Cameras were very much in evidence and the visit was captured for posterity by Gaumont British News with an item entitled 'King visits the Dambusters'. As the newsreel begins, Guy is seen standing stiffly to attention, blinking in the sunlight. He looks very smart, more so than usual, and has obviously just been under the barber's scissors. His haircut is so severe that in some shots he appears almost bald.

After speaking to the men, which included the ground crews, the King can be seen walking back towards the buildings, accompanied by Guy with his rolling gait, almost like that of a sailor. Having reached the offices once more, Guy is seen explaining to the King how the squadron carried out the attack. His explanation was assisted by the use of the models of the dams and the King was very interested in what he had to say and asked several questions.

Curiously enough Guy had, upon learning of His Majesty's visit, taken advice as to how much information he could impart to the royal visitors. Even with the raid over Guy was still very concerned with the security of the operation and was not prepared to disclose details to anyone, not even his King, without first obtaining permission.

During the Royal visit Guy showed the King two drafts of proposed badges for 617 Squadron. The first showed a hammer parting chains which were attached to a figure representing Europe. The motto beneath was 'Alter the Map.' The second, which was the one ultimately chosen, shows a breached dam with the motto 'Après moi le déluge' and symbols of lightning above the dam.

37. Guy being presented with a silver model of a Lancaster by Mr. T. Sopwith, director of A.V. Roe, during the party at the Hungaria restaurant on 22nd June, 1943. *(Derrick Warren)*

38. Guy sitting in a poppy field reading Mallory's *Morte d'Arthur*. *(via Janet de Gaynesford)*

39. De Havilland Mosquito en route to Germany, September, 1944. (*Hawker-Siddeley*)

40. Crash site of Mosquito KB267 in Steenbergen, Holland, in which Guy Gibson was killed on the night of 19 September, 1944. (*Jan van den Driesschen*)

41. Guy with Air Minister, Sir Archibald Sinclair on 3 September, 1944. On the left is A/Cmdre A.C.H. Sharpe. This is probably the last photo taken of Guy before his death on 19 September, 1944. (*Imperial War Museum*)

42. The entrance to the Roman Catholic cemetery in Steenbergen as it was at the time of Guy Gibson's burial. (*Lex de Herder*)

43. Crew of 61 Squadron Lancaster who heard Guy report he had lost an engine after successfully acting as Master Bomber on his final operation on 19 September, 1944. This photo was taken the following day and marked the 30th operation of the crew's mid-upper gunner, eighteen year old John Aldridge, front left. (*John Aldridge*)

44. The cross marking the grave of Guy Gibson and Jim Warwick has now been amended to show Guy's rank and decorations and his name has been placed above that of Jim Warwick.
(Jan van den Driesschen)

45. Local Dutch people paying their respects at the grave of Guy Gibson and Jim Warwick at Steenbergen Roman Catholic Cemetery, during the 1970s. Arrowed is Pastor J.K. van den Brink, who conducted the funeral service in 1944. .
(*Jan van den Driesschen*)

46. Guy's sister, Joan Stiles, makes her first visit to her brothers grave in August, 1992. (*A. de Herder*)

DEDICATED TO THE MEMORY OF
W/CDR GUY GIBSON
V.C. D.S.O. D.F.C. R.A.F.
617 SQDN. THE DAMBUSTERS
ON THE 45TH ANNIVERSARY
OF HIS DEATH
TUESDAY 19TH SEPTEMBER 19

47. Guy's cousin, Janet de Gaynesford, unveiling the memorial to Guy

Much has been written in the years following the raid on the Ruhr dams about the actual effect it had on the German war effort. It has been said that, although it took thousands of men months to clear up and repair the devastation, the damage caused by the raid was not sufficient to warrant the loss of so many aircrew. Others strenuously defend the operation, claiming that it was entirely justified. One fact cannot be disputed. The war had been a part of everyday life for three and a half years. People were weary and needed something to lift their spirits. As a morale booster the raid was second to none, not just for the British people but for their allies as well. People as far apart as America and Russia celebrated when they heard the news of the breaching of the dams. The authorities were quick to realize that this boost could be extended, long after the floods had subsided, by calling attention to the crews who had taken part and, more especially, to the leader of the operation.

Guy, therefore, found he had become a celebrity almost overnight. Even before the award of his Victoria Cross had been announced, he was in demand for appearances at fund-raising activities. The *Sheffield Telegraph* ran an article on 28 May advising its readers that the following day Sheffield would be privileged to welcome, not only Mrs Winston Churchill but also 'the man of the moment in the air war' Wing Commander Guy Gibson. Guy arrived in Sheffield that evening and went directly to Riverdale Grange, Fulwood, where he was the guest of Lord and Lady Riverdale. A photo of Guy and his host and hostess appeared on the front page of the *Sheffield Telegraph* the next morning, Saturday, 29 May.

Before the start of the Wings week parade Guy accompanied Mrs Churchill to a lunch given by the Lord Mayor at the City Hall. Here Guy was given a pocket knife of Sheffield steel by the chairman of the savings committee, Mr Ashley S. Ward. In her speech marking the start of the fund-raising Mrs Churchill introduced Guy and said that she was sure there was not any woman of her own age in the hall who would not be glad and proud if he were her son. These sentiments must have been especially poignant to Guy, given his background, but he smiled broadly while the audience gave him a standing ovation.

Guy began his speech by telling the assembled company that he had been to Sheffield before but had not had such a welcome that time. He explained that his previous visit had been as a fighter pilot during December, 1940, when the city had suffered its worst bombing and said, 'I had the displeasure of watching your city burn and I knew then the time would come when we would do the same to them on a much bigger scale. We always say we Britons can take it, but we can also give it.' He continued that Bomber Command was hammering the heart of Germany and that, if it continued to do so, the German people would soon be unable to take any more. He agreed with what Mrs Churchill had said about a bombing raid being more like a battle and compared the 6000 men which he said were sometimes involved in a single raid with the equivalent number of soldiers landing on the French coast. In his view that would definitely be regarded as a battle and he wanted people to realize that airmen were doing just as much as the soldiers to make their presence felt to the enemy. He stressed the need for more money to make more munitions and concluded by saying that he would like to see everyone, young and old alike, working to make the world a better place in which to live, once peace had been achieved.

Less than two weeks after the raid Guy was standing on the saluting base with Mrs Churchill, Air Commodore J. G. Murray and the Lord Mayor of Sheffield, Councillor H. E. Bridgwater, taking the salute as the parade passed in front of a crowd of over 3000. It was a position which, a few months before, he would never have imagined would be his fate. He tackled this new role, however, with characteristic enthusiasm and thoroughness and did not seem at all fazed by the crowds and the attention he was receiving.

Even after Guy had left Sheffield and gone on to London to receive his Victoria Cross, stories were still appearing in the Sheffield newspapers about him. A report on 1 June told a story of the superintendant of Sheffield town hall, Mr E. A. Beasley. This gentleman had watched the blitz in 1940 from a balcony in the town hall tower. He saw not only German bombers, but also two British fighters, but when he told his story no one believed that there were any British planes about that night. Having heard in Guy's speech that he had flown over Sheffield and seen it burn Mr Beasley felt his story must now be accepted. An unimportant little story perhaps, but it does illustrate how the media were making good use of every column inch they could squeeze from the newest holder of the Victoria Cross.

On 25 May the *Maidstone Gazette* announced that Guy would be taking part in their 'Wings for Victory' week to be held in June. They were also at pains to point out that, although Guy was not a Kent man by birth, he did have strong links with the county, having been educated in Folkestone.

For Guy the trip down to Maidstone gave him the chance to renew old friendships. Group Captain Colbeck-Welch had also been invited to take part in the Wings week, as had Guy's old scouting friend, Glad Bincham.

The week of activities began on Saturday, 19 June with a lunch at The Royal Star hotel and continued with a grand parade. Guy watched as the crowds were treated to a flypast of three Lancasters. The aircraft were piloted by Micky Martin, David Maltby and Dave Shannon and the display was rather unusual in that the three aircraft were flying on only six of their twelve engines. Micky Martin led the flight using his two inner engines. On his left was David Maltby flying on his two port and on his right was David Shannon using his two starboard engines.

The following evening The Royal Star was the venue for an auction conducted by comedian Richard Hearne. Guy had been billed to assist the 'auctioneer' but remained in the audience, claiming it was against King's Regulations to take part in such an event. This prompted the comment from Richard Hearne, 'I understood that Wing Commander Gibson was going to help me with the sale, but I am glad he is not. He would probably have made an awful mess of it. Look what he did to the Ruhr!'

In spite of Guy's lack of assistance the auction was a success and raised £4800. The largest single sum was £1000 paid for two bottles of whisky, a bottle of gin and a bottle of sherry which had been donated by Glad Bincham. Guy donated a bottle of Liebfraumilch, which he autographed and this was sold, along with six rolls of wallpaper, for £600!

Earlier that day Guy had been to visit the 1st Tovil troop where Glad was scoutmaster. Guy had been a scout as a boy and had expressed a desire to 're-muster' as he put it, as a Rover scout. This he did that afternoon along with Group Captain E. Colbeck-Welch, DFC, Wing Commander S. P. Richards, AFC, Flight Lieutenant K. Davison and Lieutenant F. Carruthers, RA. He spoke afterwards of his time in the scouts as a boy and admitted that the only badge he had attempted was the cook's badge. He also told the scout troop that his membership of the movement had taught him the decent things in life – resourcefulness, courage and devotion to duty.

When he spoke a little later in London at the Boy Scout Association's annual meeting he said, 'I, for one, hope we are not going to be too lenient with the Germans after the war. The young super goose-stepping Nazi brought up to the Nazi creed from the age of three, who hates everything except arrogance and cruelty, is going to be hard to re-educate. It will take much washing to make him clean.'

Two days after re-joining the Scouts, Guy was once again at a ceremony, this time at Buckingham Palace where he collected a bar to his DSO and the Victoria Cross.

The citation for the award of the Victoria Cross was quite long and detailed Guy's career up to date. It spoke of his outstandingly successful results, both as a pilot and as a leader and stated that his courage knew no bounds. With regard to the raid on the Ruhr dams, for which Guy had received the award, the citation said:

'Under his inspiring leadership this squadron has now executed one of the most devastating attacks of the war – the breaching of the Möhne and Eder dams.

'The task was fraught with danger and difficulty. Wing Commander Gibson personally made the initial attack on the Möhne dam. Descending to within a few feet of the water and taking the full brunt of the anti-aircraft defences, he launched his projectiles with great accuracy. Afterwards he circled very low for thirty minutes, drawing the enemy fire on himself in order to leave as free a run as possible to the following aircraft which were attacking the dam in turn.'

The citation continued with a completely inaccurate statement that Guy had used the same decoy tactics at the Eder dam and then concluded:

'Wing Commander Gibson has completed over 170 sorties, involving more than 600 hours operational flying. Throughout his operational career, prolonged exceptionally at his own request, he has shown leadership, determination and valour of the highest order.'

Eve Gibson accompanied her husband to Buckingham Palace, the fourth time she had made such a trip. As the King was on a visit to the troops in North Africa, the investiture was conducted by the Queen. Her own standard flew over the Palace on the morning of 22 June and she stood alone, in a grey costume trimmed with pink orchids, as she presented the awards to 617 Squadron and over 200 others.

Guy received his two awards first, followed by the other

members of his Squadron in alphabetical order. The Queen chatted to all the recipients, remembering many of their names from her visit to Scampton the previous month. Eve, sitting close to the front, strained her ears to hear what the Queen was saying to Guy but was unsuccessful.

Outside the Palace the press was waiting to pounce. Photographs were taken and another newsreel captured Guy proudly marching, with his Squadron around him. As soon as he was able, Guy escaped back to his hotel room where he was interviewed by a *Daily Mirror* reporter who said in his article that the man who had braved the raid on the dams was afraid to face the crowds waiting to welcome him outside the Palace. Guy did admit that he was glad it was all over. His relief was more due to tiredness than to fear of the crowds. Since the middle of May he had done little else but face large crowds and was becoming quite used to being regarded as a celebrity.

At the age of 24 Guy Gibson had become the most highly decorated man of the entire war. The neglected little boy with the lofty ambitions had surpassed even his own expectations. He had made a success of his life, in spite of all the problems of his youth. Who could blame him for feeling proud of his achievements?

On the evening of the investiture a party was given by A. V. Roe and Co. at the Hungaria restaurant in London's Lower Regent Street. Many, but not all, 617 Squadron members were present. They had mostly travelled down from Lincolnshire together by train and the atmosphere during the journey was that of a party. The silly tricks usually reserved for the Mess were performed on the train, leaving the other passengers to wonder what on earth was happening. After the ceremony at Buckingham Palace some of them went off to celebrations of their own. Others had intended to attend the party but had been detained by their families and friends or by well-wishers in the pubs to which some of them had retired. It was said that in the days after the raid no member of 617 Squadron was permitted to pay for anything whilst in London – drinks, taxi rides, all were provided free.

Those who were present at the party received a menu card on which they were described as 'Damn Busters.' This was discovered later not to be a deliberate pun but rather the work of someone who was very bad at spelling. The cards were put to good use during the evening, however, being used to collect the autographs of the many distinguished guests, who included Roy Chadwick, designer of the Lancaster who had been given the CBE, and Barnes Wallis. Mr Chadwick said at the party that he was very proud to have been decorated with the boys of 617.

During the course of the evening, an enlarged copy of the photograph taken by Flying Officer Fray was auto-graphed by the Squadron members present and was presented to Barnes Wallis. It was later to adorn a wall in his office.

Guy was presented with a silver model of a Lancaster by A. V. Roe's director Mr T. Sopwith, who also placed the highest bid in the auction which was held that evening, for a fusing link from the first bomb to be dropped on the dams. This item raised £30 and the proceeds went to the RAF Benevolent Fund. Guy was asked to make a speech during which he said, 'Well, chaps, we have had a lot of praise, but this raid was not carried out by one man. It was carried out by a lot of people working hard.' Then he and the other aircrew raised their glasses to the ground crews present and sang 'For they are jolly good fellows'.

Life for the 'Dambusters' gradually got back to normal. They returned to Scampton where some continued with 617 Squadron while others were posted. Guy did not fly again after the raid until the beginning of July as he was still busy in his public relations role.

The workers at the aircraft factories were not forgotten

and Guy, with some of his crews, visited the A. V. Roe works at Chadderton to talk to and thank the people who had built the Lancaster bomber. As a souvenir of the visit, postcards were produced which showed a Lancaster in flight surrounded by the signatures of Guy and the other officers. These were sold for 6d in aid of war funds.

Visits to other establishments followed and Guy was often asked to say a few words. He was even booked to give talks to various groups, including the Women's Institute. At one such event, now quite well known, Guy was introduced to the ladies by the chairwoman. She was quite flustered at having such a well known guest speaker and introduced him as 'Wing Commander Gibson, the famous bomb duster.' Guy was very amused by this slip and pulled a handkerchief from his pocket and pretended to dust, much to the delight of the ladies present.

On 12 July he made a visit to the Trent Lane head-quarters of the ATC in Nottingham. Here he presented the Captain Albert Ball Victoria Cross Sword of Honour to Flight Sergeant Penniston. This was an especially proud moment for Guy, as Albert Ball had been his childhood hero.

At the end of July Guy was invited, along with Eve, to spend the day with Winston Churchill at Chequers. When they arrived they were greeted by the Prime Minister who immediately whisked Guy off to the garden to help him with one of his building projects. The luncheon party consisted of eight men, Mrs Churchill and Eve. During the afternoon Guy's hatred of the Nazi system was reinforced when he and Eve were shown a film which had, somehow, been brought from Germany and showed the atrocities being committed at Hitler's concentration camps. Before the couple left Chequers Mr Churchill hinted that he had plans to extend Guy's public relations role, possibly to include a trip overseas.

Chapter 9

THE BEST AMBASSADOR

True to his word, Winston Churchill did have plans for Guy. On 27 July, 1943, Guy went down to London on 'temporary duty'. The nature of this duty was soon revealed. Guy was to accompany the Prime Minister on Operation Quadrant, the code name for the Quebec Conference.

The journey began on platform ten of King's Cross station in London on 4 August. Very specific instructions had been given to all members of the Prime Minister's party about their travel arrangements. There was a confusing array of rules about who paid for what on board the train. For example, no dinner had been provided on the evening of 4 August, but anyone who so desired was free to purchase their own drinks. The following morning breakfast would be provided, free of charge, by courtesy of the War Cabinet office. They would also pay for the gratuities for the restaurant car staff, but sleeping car staff tips were the responsibilities of the individual.

The train departed just before midnight on its way to Faslane in Scotland and arrived just over 14 hours later, in the early afternoon of 5 August.

During the train journey the passengers were provided with passes which they had to keep with them at all times. These were colour coded and, instead of the person's name, had a code number for security reasons. The numerical part of the code was the cabin number on board the ship which would take them to Canada. Guy's code number was S27. This number had also to be used on baggage tags. Passengers were warned to take only a small amount of baggage as it had to be easily handled by the ship's crews, who would load it in the appropriate cabins.

Passports were not necessary for anyone in the official party and arrangements were made for the authorities in Canada and in the USA to honour the passes held by the party and to facilitate a swift completion of formalities upon arrival.

A great many people accompanied the Prime Minister, both staff and guests, representing the three services. Amongst the better known personalities were Lord Louis Mountbatten and Air Chief Marshal Sir Charles Portal, Chief of the Air Staff. Mrs Churchill accompanied her husband as did their daughter, Mary.

After all the party had boarded the ship, lunch was served and RMS *Queen Mary* set sail for Halifax, Nova Scotia.

If Guy had imagined that the trip would be a complete rest he was mistaken. He was not able to relax as much as he would have liked as there were so many 'top brass' also on board. Towards the end of the voyage, on 8 August, he was asked to give a lecture about his experiences.

Although most people acknowledged that it was an excellent talk, given without the benefit of notes, Guy made two remarks which caused some concern and about which he was spoken to by Winston Churchill himself.

The first remark was that when the bombers went on a big raid to a target such as Bremen, they did not worry too much about placing their bombs on military targets. In Guy's own words: 'We just plunk them down in the middle of the town.' His other remark which worried some members of the party concerned the aftermath of the Dams raid. Guy described the torrent of water which gushed from the breach in the Möhne dam and said: 'There must have been a great many casualties, and a good job too!'

It was felt that these two remarks, if made in a talk in Canada or the USA, would shock people and would do damage to Britain's credibility. The people of these countries had not suffered in the way Britons had suffered. They had not been bombed night after night and, it was supposed, would not understand the feelings of British people when it came to bombing Germany. Mr Churchill, when he spoke to Guy, asked him to tone down this type of remark so as not to offend anyone.

When the ship docked at Halifax the party were once more put on to a special train to take them on the last stage of their journey to Quebec. Guy was given a sleeper in compartment D, more highly regarded than some of the party who were obliged to sleep in their seats.

Arriving, at last, in Quebec City, Guy found that the conference party had taken up almost the entire accommodation at the famous Château Frontenac hotel. This had provided the manager, Mr Neal, with some slight problems. Living at the hotel were a number of elderly people, including Miss Alice Caron who had had an apartment there since 1918. Her doctor was most concerned at the prospect of her having to be moved and so an exception was made and she was allowed to stay among the conference party. The party took over 624 rooms and the whole arrangement cost the Canadian government $8000 a day. Guy's room was number 3515 and was situated on the fifth floor.

A newspaper report on Wednesday, 11 August described Guy as a shy young man with a pleasant and easy-going manner. Most people who knew Guy would not have described him as shy; quite the opposite in fact. Two days later he was introduced to the press by Mr C. G. Power, the Canadian Air Minister, at a press conference held at the Clarendon Hotel. Here he was able to explain how this misunderstanding had occurred.

At the end of his first day in Canada, he was getting ready for bed when he had a phone call to say that a reporter was coming up to see him. He readily agreed to see the man and said he would have a drink waiting for him. He took out a bottle and two glasses and was just getting in to bed when the door opened, and in walked the reporter. 'He' was a rather attractive blonde and for a moment Guy was speechless. The reporter was so amused that this great war hero could be so shocked that she wrote the story about his shyness.

Having cleared up this false impression Guy went on to tell the members of the press the purpose of his visit to Canada. He explained that he would be touring the country speaking to men at air training camps describing what it was like to fly on raids over Germany. These men would not all be Canadians as many of the would-be pilots were taking part in what was known as the British Commonwealth Air Training Plan and came from all over the Empire. It was felt that a talk from someone who had actually been through what these trainee pilots were about to experience would be of great benefit to their confidence and morale.

The reporters asked Guy about his own experiences and he told them that it was the luck of the draw that he was there at all and certainly had nothing to do with any skill on his part. Most of the reporters, knowing what he had been through on the night of 16/17 May that year, refused to believe that.

He was, of course, questioned about the Dams raid, but did not want to say too much about it except that it was the skill of the bomber crews involved and the genius of British engineering that had made the whole thing possible. Asked from where the idea to attack the Dams had come, Guy said that they had been regarded as a military target since the beginning of the war. A story had been circulating that the idea had come from a German Jewish refugee but this was simply not true.

By the time Guy had been in Canada for a little more than a week, the Canadian authorities were anxious for him to begin his lecture tour and permission was sought from the Prime Minister for him to be released from his party. This was duly given and he began what was to become a very gruelling yet enjoyable tour.

One of his first public appearances took him to the No. 8 Air Observer school at L'Ancienne Lorette, near Quebec City. Here he was introduced to the pupils by the CO of the school, Wing Commander G. W. Jacobi who spoke in English. Squadron Leader Guy Vadeboncoeur, the Officer Commanding No. 1 Air Gunnery Ground Training School then repeated the introduction, this time in French.

In his talk Guy told the pupils that navigators were rapidly taking the place of the pilot as the 'main man' in a bomber crew. He didn't like to say this as he was a pilot himself, but it was true. He told them how the members of his Squadron spent their spare time looking at the stars and trying to find a reliable way of navigating at low level. He urged them to do the same when they eventually joined their squadrons.

A few days later at a Wings parade, also near Quebec City, he presented wings to graduate navigators. They came from all over the country, together with men from other air forces, including the Royal Norwegian Air Force Naval Service.

Having begun his tour close to the point of his arrival in Canada, Guy then started his journey, zig-zagging across the country. He went from Quebec City to Montreal and Ottawa, flying in a Lockheed 12 with the Canadian First World War ace, Air Vice-Marshal Bishop VC. Then on to Toronto, London and Jarvis before returning to Toronto from where he made an overnight trip to New York before returning to Toronto once more to hold a press conference.

Those who attended this press conference were amazed at the confidence shown by Guy in his handling of the press. As with everything he did, he tackled the press with a determination to get it right and did not allow anyone to divert him from this aim. Asked, inevitably, about the raid on the Ruhr dams Guy told the reporters that his own safety had not occurred to him as he was just thinking about the success of the mission. He thought that all pilots would react this way and do anything they could to ensure a favourable conclusion to a raid.

In the reports that were printed of this press conference, Guy was described as being unaffected and sincere. It was also thought that he did not take himself or his exploits too seriously and that, when he spoke, a pleasant sense of humour was in evidence. As a Rover Scout Guy wore a Scout wristband, similar in appearance to a watch. When he was asked by a reporter why he wore a watch on each wrist he did not tell him that one was a Scout wristband. Instead he said with a grin, 'This one looks good and the other one tells the time accurately!'

By the end of the first week of September, Guy's journey had taken him on to Winnepeg, Yorkton, Moose-jaw, Dafoe, Mossbank and finally to Calgary in Alberta where he arrived on 11 September. Most of his journeys were by air, flying in aircraft of the Royal Canadian Air Force and occasionally with the national airline, TCA. On many of the former Guy piloted himself. The remainder of his travels were by train, which gave him a chance to see something of the countryside. He was amazed at the size of Canada and enjoyed very much the journeys across the vast prairies.

Although he had been enthusiastically welcomed wherever he went, the reception he received at Calgary surpassed any that had gone before. For many days before his arrival there had been publicity about his trip and a route taking him from the airfield at Currie to the Palliser Hotel had been carefully planned so that as many people as possible would be able to turn out and greet him. The entire route was published in the daily newspaper, the *Calgary Herald*, twice in the days leading up to the visit, as the organizers did not want anyone to miss Guy's arrival.

When Guy's aeroplane taxied to a standstill at No. 3 SFTS at Currie he jumped out to be greeted by crowds of cheering people. An official welcoming party consisting of Air Force and civic officials had been organized. Guy was met by the AOC No. 3 SFTS, Wing Commander W. R. Irwin, AVM G. R. Howsam MC, AOC No. 4 Training Command and the Mayor of Calgary, Andrew Davison. He was whisked away from the crowds almost immediately and taken to the control tower, from where he made a short broadcast over the CFCN radio station. Guy had been expected to talk about his 'dambusting' exploits, but said very little on this subject. The Calgary residents, listening to the broadcast, were delighted when he spoke instead of the great job being done by Canadian pilots and crews. He impressed everyone with his modesty and unwillingness to talk about himself. They were even more impressed when they saw how young he was; one person commented that Guy looked as if he had yet to reach his 20th birthday. He had, in fact, celebrated his 25th birthday shortly after his arrival in Quebec City.

Waiting to meet Guy at the control tower was Mrs J. Taerum, mother of Guy's navigator on the Dam's raid, Harlo 'Terry' Taerum. She was a Calgary resident and had been looking forward to hearing from Guy first-hand information about her son. Guy recognized Mrs Taerum immediately, saying that she was the image of Terry or rather that Terry was the image of her. He told her he was 'awfully glad' to meet her.

In his welcoming address AVM Howsam told Guy that everyone was looking forward to hearing what he had to say about bombing Germany. Very shortly the students he would be talking to would be 'Dam busting, Cologne busting, Hamburg busting and finally busting Hitler's phoney fortress of Europe'. Guy, in his reply, said that this was the first welcome of this type that he had had since arriving in Canada and he deeply appreciated it. He thanked everyone for 'coming out to have a look at me!'

After dinner that evening Guy made another broadcast over the *Calgary Herald* radio station, CFAC. When asked what he thought of Canadian flyers he replied that they were no different from the English, New Zealanders or any others. They were all good men fighting under the same flag against the same enemy. He concluded by saying, 'We're all damn good – that's why we're winning this war!'

The following evening, Sunday, 12 September, Guy had been invited to Mrs Taerum's home where he spent several hours chatting with her about Terry. She said later that Guy was one of the nicest people she had ever met and that their meeting was one of the proudest and happiest moments of her life. Guy reminded her very much of her own son. Their builds were similar, as were their cheerful, natural manners. Three nights later Mrs Taerum's son, Flying Officer Harlo Taerum, was killed. The news reached Canada on 20 September by which time Guy was in Montreal. He was, of course, distressed by the news and said that Terry had been a great boy and a great navigator.

During Guy's brief visit to Calgary he also had the opportunity of meeting LAC Robert Young of Pasadena, California. LAC Young, although an American citizen, was training at No. 2 Wireless School as he intended to join the Royal Air Force and follow in the footsteps of his brother, Squadron Leader Melvyn Young, who had been killed over the Dams on the night of 16–17 May that year. Guy encouraged the 20-year-old by telling him that pilots were not everything and that the other members of a bomber crew had just as important parts to play.

Leaving Calgary, Guy completed the next part of his journey, to Vancouver, by train, arriving on 13 September at the Canadian Pacific railway station. Here he was met by the Mayor of Vancouver, Mr J. W. Cornett and Air Commodore A. H. Hull, acting AOC, Western Air Command. From the station he was driven in an open car to the Hotel Vancouver where he stayed for two days. On the last part of the car ride he was accompanied by the drum and bugle band of the Royal Canadian Air Force and was, once more, cheered by a large crowd as he stepped from the car. One onlooker was so impressed by Guy's medals that he said he thought they were equal to two Victoria Crosses.

One of the main events of Guy's visit to Vancouver was when he addressed 300 air cadets from schools in Vancouver and New Westminster. They stood to attention as Guy inspected them and told them he hoped they would soon be flying with him. He spoke of the war with Japan and said he had heard stories of the way the Japanese treated their prisoners of war. He was very anxious to be involved with the defeat of Japan. He then told the cadets that it was up to them and their generation once the war was over to ensure that another war did not happen. He thought the way to make this certain was to have united nations and free trade, a solution showing all the insight of a modern politician.

Three times during the course of his talk, Guy had to pause while cadets, standing stiffly to attention, fainted. Guy was very sympathetic and told them that they should not worry about it as it had also happened to him.

He concluded his talk by telling the cadets that ground crews were just as important as those who fly. He stressed the importance of each member of the team and told them that flying was no longer regarded as a glamorous occupation.

The most important event to happen in Vancouver for Guy himself was the day he was given the freedom of the City of Vancouver and was presented with a medal to commemorate the occasion.

When the time came to leave Vancouver Guy piloted himself in a Grumman Goose on the short flight to Victoria where he spent two days before taking a scheduled TCA fight from Victoria back to Montreal. Flying as a passen-

133

ger, he was able to sit back and enjoy the flight, one of whose attractions was descried by Guy in his logbook as 'One Very Nice Air Hostess'.

In Montreal he spoke to students at No. 1 Wireless School and at the headqurters of No. 3 Training Command before addressing the Royal Air Force Veterans Association at a dinner held at the Mount Royal Hotel.

At this event he told the veterans that victory was certain, but that he was not convinced that Germany could be bombed out of the war. He felt that the bombing would soften the country and could destroy its industry, but that it would take more than the bombing to end the war. Guy spoke confidently in front of an audience, comprising not only US cadet officers, but many Air Vice-Marshals, Lieutenant-Colonels, Colonels and Commanders as well as the President of the Veterans Association. The room in which the function was held was decorated with a replica of a Lancaster bomber and the guests were entertained by the band of the Royal Canadian Air Force.

Guy finished his Canadian tour at the end of September with trips to Bagotville, Mont Jolie, Halifax, Greenbridge, Petrie and Monkton. Returning briefly to Montreal, he went on to Ottawa where he stayed at the Seignory Club for a few days, as he put it 'to recover'.

The second part of Guy's North American tour began at the beginning of October when, piloting himself in a Lockheed 12, he flew from Ottawa to Washington, DC. The American part of the trip was just as hectic as the Canadian visit and in the first two weeks of October he visited Pittsburgh, Kansas City, Orlando, Morrison, Miami and New York.

In New York he gave an interview at the offices of the British Information Services at Rockefeller Plaza before going on to a shopping trip in Manhattan. Eve Gibson was delighted a few days later to receive a parcel via the Air Ministry containing clothes which Guy had bought for her at Gimbels, the well-known New York department store.

On 13 October he returned to Washington to receive an award. This had been granted by President Roosevelt when he had met Guy earlier and was presented to him by General 'Hap' Arnold, Commander-in-Chief of the United States Army Air Force. The award was the Commander's Insignia to the Legion of Merit, one of the highest decorations given in the USA. Very few foreign nationals were honoured in this way and Guy shared this distinction with only two other British men, General Alexander and the then General Sir Bernard Montgomery.

After this brief respite from his lecture tour Guy returned to public speaking, talking to people from places as far afield as Pittsburgh, Chicago, Minneapolis, Burbank and San Francisco.

In Hollywood Guy mixed with movie stars and directors. He stayed for two weeks at the home of director Howard Hawks and his wife and thoroughly enjoyed the company of actors. He said that, while they were good company, he would hate to have been an actor as it would be much too nerve-racking.

One evening, while visiting the Legion Stadium on El Centro Avenue in Hollywood for a boxing match, he was spotted in the crowd. He was introduced to the audience who gave him a three-minute standing ovation. Asked to say a few words to the crowd, Guy told them that, 'It is my ambition and that of everyone in the RAF to get to the Pacific and bomb hell out of the little yellow bellies!' The crowd cheered even louder at these remarks. The incident was reported in all the local newspapers and it was agreed that Guy was the best ambassador ever sent by Great Britain to the USA.

By the time he left Hollywood, having had an exhausting but enjoyable stay, his tour was almost over. He took a Western Airlines aeroplane to San Francisco where he stayed for a few days at the Palace Hotel before flying on to New York. From there he went back to Ottawa in Canada.

The time he had spent in North America was a little under three months, but during that time he had made over 150 speeches, many of them broadcast over the wireless. There were many newspaper reports, most of them dealing with the Dams raid. All of them, however, agreed that Guy was a wonderful ambassador for his country and that he was a thoroughly nice, modest young man with a good sense of humour. He had been fêted wherever he went, receiving the sort of acclaim usually reserved for heads of state or film stars. When he boarded the aeroplane which was to bring him back to war-torn England, he did so in the knowledge that his trip had been an outstanding success.

On 1 December, 1943, Guy left Montreal in a Consolidated Liberator bound for Prestwick, near Glasgow, leaving behind Canada, which he had grown to love and the Canadian people who had grown to love him.

Chapter 10

PUBLIC RELATIONS AND POLITICS

When Guy's aeroplane arrived back on British soil at Prestwick Airport he was near to collapse. The lecture tour had taken away his last reserves of strength and he was exhausted. The long hours, parades, receptions, speeches and the thousands of miles he had flown during the three months he had been away had taken their toll. His face was pale and had lost its boyish chubbiness and there were dark circles under his eyes. The day after his return from Canada he was admitted to the RAF hospital at Rauceby. He was suffering from Vincent's angina, an extremely painful, ulcerative inflammation of the throat.

He had been due to go on a course on 6 December at the RAF Staff College at Gerrards Cross in Buckinghamshire, but this was cancelled when it was found that he was too ill to attend and he remained in hospital at Rauceby until 17 December. Although Guy found his enforced stay in hospital irritating it did, at least, give him a chance to have a complete rest and he emerged from the hospital, just before Christmas, feeling much better.

Despite the fact that his health was improving he was still not fit enough to return to flying and so another job had to be found for him. This was as a staff officer at the Air Ministry, Directorate of Accidents, to which establishment he was posted on 3 January, 1944. It was not, of course, to his liking but there was nothing he could do about it.

During the time spent at the Air Ministry Guy was asked if he would write a book about his RAF experiences. In much the same way as when he had lectured in Canada and the USA, it was felt that his story would be a source of inspiration to both novice and experienced air crew. So it was that *Enemy Coast Ahead* came into being. It has been suggested by some that Guy did not actually write this book but that it was 'ghosted' for him by some anonymous person. Those who knew him well categorically refute this suggestion and it seems almost certain that the book is his own work. It carries the hallmark of his sense of humour and is a fine book, praised by one critic as being 'one of the great true stories of World War II'.

Writing a book is very time-consuming and it was while Guy was busy at this that he suddenly found demands on his time from a completely different direction. Shortly after the raid on the Ruhr dams, when he had been making a lot of public appearances, Guy was introduced to Mr Garfield Weston, MP.

Willard Garfield Weston was a Canadian citizen who had come to live in England in 1934. He was a business-man, who in his home town of Toronto, had been the manager of the family company George Weston Ltd. After his arrival in Britain, Garfield Weston, as he was usually known, founded the Weston Biscuit Company which had branches all over the country. He later went on to start the giant food company Allied Bakeries.

In 1939 Garfield Weston had become the Conservative Member of Parliament for Macclesfield and it was in his parliamentary capacity that he contacted Guy early in 1944. He had decided that, because of his business com-mitments, he would be unable to continue in Parliament after the war and was looking for someone suitable to take his place. When he had met Guy in 1943, Mr Weston had been impressed with the young pilot's courage, determination and honesty and had decided that perhaps he would be a possible candidate.

When Guy thought of what he would be doing after the war, something connected with flying was usually upper-most in his mind. He had, after all, joined the RAF to learn to fly so that he could become a test pilot. However, when Garfield Weston broached the subject of politics, Guy was interested. He had very definite ideas about how post-war Britain should be governed and was very keen that people from his own generation should have a major part to play. He was certain of victory for the Allies and it was the men of his generation who would be winning the war. It seemed only fair that they should be able to benefit from this victory.

Deciding to find out more about the possibilities of serving in Parliament, Guy, accompanied by Eve, went to Mr Weston's country house at Marlow, Buckinghamshire, in February, 1944. It was a foggy day and the train journey took hours longer than normal. The weekend was a great success, however, and both Guy and Eve enjoyed the company of Mr Weston and his family. Eight of the MP's nine children were at home that weekend and all except the youngest two could play a musical instrument. They had formed their own orchestra and kept their guests entertained with their performances when their father was not busy talking to Guy about his political aspirations.

The discussions went well and Guy decided to accept the challenge should it be offered to him. The next step was to go to Macclesfield. Although Mr Weston was backing Guy, it was by no means certain that he would be adopted by the local party and it was important for him to make himself known in the area. Eve went with him, although she was not pleased to be told by Guy that she would have to be vetted by the chairman of the local Conservative party. When she asked what she should do, Guy's only reply was 'Nothing, and for God's sake, don't sing!'

A very full programme had been arranged in Macclesfield. Garfield Weston gave a dinner in honour of Lord Vansittart at the Macclesfield Arms Hotel. He was a former Under-Secretary at the Foreign Office and had then become a chief diplomatic adviser. He was visiting

Macclesfield in his capacity as chairman of the 'Win the Peace' movement and was accompanied by Lady Vansittart. Guy and Eve were included as part of Lord Vansittart's party and this generated a lot of publicity.

Always escorted by Garfield Weston, Guy was taken to meet the people of Macclesfield. He attended dinners and receptions and was invited to speak at the Civil Defence Headquarters in the town. Eve was amazed by his speech. He spoke clearly and confidently and used no notes. When she congratulated him afterwards, he laughingly replied that he had not spent three months in Canada and the USA for nothing. His North American trip had given him the practice he would need in speech-making if he were to become an MP. The people of Macclesfield were also impressed by what Guy said and he was given a standing ovation as he left the room.

His speeches were not controversial. He spoke of his hopes for the country once the war had been won and stated his desire to ensure that the troops were given a fair deal in housing and jobs when they returned home. What he thought, but was tactful enough not to say in public was that the country needed young men such as himself in government to ensure that another war would not be allowed to happen. He felt quite strongly that it was time to oust the older politicians and industrialists who, he felt, had without compunction sent thousands of young men to their deaths.

Guy wanted to meet the working people of the area as well as the dignitaries and was invited to tour the premises of Edmund Lomas Ltd., a silk manufacturer. Macclesfield was, at this time, the centre of silk production in the United Kingdom. Guy spent over two hours at the factory being shown the processes of silk production and speaking to many of the workers.

The final visit during his time in Macclesfield was one in which he felt quite at home. Garfield Weston, his secretary Mr Butler, and Eve and Guy were taken to an aircraft factory in the Manchester area where they saw Lancaster bombers being built and Guy was, once more, able to speak to the workers, who gave him a rousing reception. A treat was also in store for Eve and the MP and his secretary. Guy took them for a short flight around the area and they were able to get some small insight into what it was like to fly the big bomber.

The week before his visit to Macclesfield Guy had been invited by the BBC to appear on *Desert Island Discs*. The programme was then only a year old and Guy was the 43rd 'castaway' to appear. The programme was recorded in London on 11 February and was broadcast the following week on Saturday, 19 February at 7.35 pm. Guy's sister Joan remembers how she and her family gathered around the wireless that winter evening to listen to her now famous brother. The programme had only been on for a few moments when a neighbour arrived and in spite of being told what Joan was listening to, talked through the entire 30 minute programme.

Guy was introduced to the audience by Roy Plomley, the inventor of the series. He spoke of a fair-haired young RAF officer who, although only 25, had already reached the rank of Wing Commander. He described him as the most highly decorated man in the British Empire and then handed the programme over to Guy, who told the listeners that he was by no means a 'highbrow' and said he knew very little about music other than the pieces that he particularly liked. Even then he had had problems with putting names to the melodies, but had been helped by Eve and by friends to whom he had hummed tunes in the hope of finding out the titles.

He began his choice with a record which he said reminded him of Mess parties in the days when he and his squadron were bombing Germany nightly. The record was *The Warsaw Concerto* and Guy said that in the Mess they would put it on the radiogram and leave it to repeat itself time and time again. The other records which reminded him of his life in the Air Force were *The RAF March*, which he said never failed to send a shiver down his spine, and *If I had my Way* sung by Bing Crosby. Guy said that he thought the latter was a wee bit corny, but that he was very attached to it. He had heard so many imitation Crosbys over the intercom when he was flying that it would be a treat to hear the real thing. This remark undoubtedly referred to his old wireless operator from both 106 and 617 Squadrons. Flight Lieutenant Hutchison had been known as 'Hutch' to his fellow crew members and friends in the RAF but his family knew him as 'Bing' because of his talent for singing like the 'Old Groaner' himself.

For his choice of more serious music Guy picked Wagner: *The Flying Dutchman* because it reminded him of the sea and his old favourite *The Ride of the Valkyries*. He said the latter reminded him of a bombing raid, although he did not think it was actually like one. He also chose a Strauss waltz, *A Thousand and One Nights*, because he had always loved Strauss. This was one of the titles he had not known and had hummed it in friends' faces and over the telephone until someone had recognized it and given him the name.

To bring back memories of what Guy described as 'one of the most exciting things that happened in my life' he picked the *Marines March – To the Shores of Tripoli*. He had first heard it at a march-past when he was in America and it would remind him of the wonderful time he spent there.

Only one record had anything to do with Guy's private life. It was what he called a cracking good dance tune and reminded him of the summer of 1940 when he and Eve were first engaged. It was the Rodgers and Hart song *Where or When* sung by Adelaide Hall, a rather sad choice in view of the problems Guy and Eve were by then experiencing.

By March Guy was, once again, back in Macclesfield.

The original list of possible candidates being considered for selection by the Conservative party there had numbered 28. During March this was narrowed down to 11 and included such names as Flight Lieutenant Aitken, a nephew of Lord Beaverbrook, and the famous Pathfinder, AVM Bennett. After more discussions the short-listed names were five and each of these was interviewed by the selection committee. The interviews eliminated one more name and the committee members then voted for two of the other four candidates.

Guy won this ballot with a vote of 23, his nearest rival, Lieutenant W. Shepherd gaining 18. In the final ballot Guy polled 17 votes, four more than Shepherd and was duly selected to be the prospective Conservative parliamentary candidate for the Macclesfield division.

Having been informed of their decision, Guy briefly addressed the committee. He told them he was very proud to have been selected and said that he looked forward, one day, to fighting all comers for the seat. Until then his loyalties remained with the RAF until victory was won.

At a press conference held later at the Macclesfield Arms Hotel Guy said that he had four reasons for wishing to stand for parliament and these were:

1. To serve any truly representative body of English men and women who do me the honour of electing me.

2. To support Mr Winston Churchill, both now and after the war, with the utmost loyalty and energy.

3. To champion in the House of Commons the interests of all members of the Forces. When they return to 'civvy street' with their multifarious problems, their welfare will be one of my paramount concerns.

4. To lend a humble hand in shaping the new Britain. Whatever the planners may devise, youth will inherit the legacy. I speak for youth. We have a right and we demand a right to have some say in moulding the country and the Empire for which youth has fought so hard.

Guy was asked if he intended to live in Macclesfield but could not say whether or not he would. He told the press that he had obtained permission from the RAF to stand as a prospective candidate and that it would not interfere with his flying career as he did not expect there to be an election until the war was over.

Garfield Weston spoke of the freshness and enthusiasm of youth which he said Guy possessed and that he had the type of drive that insisted on an answer. He concluded by saying that he thought Guy was a grand fellow and that he had the makings of a great man.

These sentiments were not shared by the Labour party in Macclesfield. At a meeting attended by Mr Emanuel Shinwell, the Labour councillor, C. J. Douthwaite said he thought that if Guy really wanted to support the serving man he should have joined the Labour party. He stated that the only positive thing he could see in the selection of Guy as prospective Conservative candidate was that it showed that the Conservative party realized the tremendous challenge being put forward by Labour and had obviously selected Guy in the hope of appealing to hero worship. Mr Shinwell wanted everyone to know that, although Guy might have been good at busting dams, he would not be able to bust the Labour party.

A few days after his selection in Macclesfield, Guy was able to go to Buckinghamshire to attend the course which he had missed after returning from Canada. The Staff college was at Bulstrode Park, Gerrard's Cross, in a fine old house which had been requisitioned by the RAF for the duration of the war. Unfortunately, not all the officers who attended the college were accommodated in the house and many had to rough it in Nissen huts. Guy shared his hut with two other officers, one a colonel in the American 8th Air Force. Although the course itself was quite interesting and there were many prominent speakers brought in to talk to the officers, Guy was eager for it to finish so that he could get back to flying.

At the end of March he was invited to Scotland to carry out two engagements with the Edinburgh Wing of the Air Training Corps. Eve accompanied him on this trip which began on 24 March with a luncheon in his honour given by the Lord Povost, Sir William Darling, at the City Chambers. The guests included RAF and civic officials, Lord and Lady Hamilton and Commissioner Lamb of the Salvation Army.

In proposing a toast to Guy the Lord Provost said, 'Wing Commander Gibson represents in a unique way the resolution, gallantry, and if I may say so, youth and grace of the RAF. We ageing earth-bound creatures look with amazement at these men who challenge the skies. The poets in the past have been poets of prophesy, but poets today cannot keep pace with the romance, the magical over-mastering courage and the beauty of this new service which embraces the vaulting genius of man untrammelled by considerations of time and space. Our guest today is an heroic figure and it is the duty of us all to honour the brave.' There followed loud and prolonged applause, broken only when Guy got to his feet to reply. His words were far less eloquent than those of the Lord Provost, but were simple and to the point. He told them that the men of the RAF were purely democratic types who had found that, by facing death together, they had got a rather nice attitude to life.

That evening he took the salute at a march-past of the Edinburgh Wing, prior to giving a lecture to the Air Training Corps at the Central Hall, Tollcross. During the lecture he showed some of his own films.

The following day he attended the Air Training Corps air pageant, held at the Empire theatre. The pageant was entitled 'Hitch your Wagon to a Star' and linked the training of the cadets of the day with man's earliest conceptions of flight. Guy was introduced to the audience by Sir William Darling.

On Sunday, 9 April the Macclesfield constituents had

their first real chance to hear the new prospective candidate speak when he appeared on the BBC Home service programme, *The Week's Good Cause*. He spoke on behalf of St Mary's Hospital in Manchester, which was concerned mainly with the health and welfare of women and children. He told the listeners that as a serviceman he could say that it meant something to a man to know that his wife and baby were to be cared for by experts. He felt this to be especially true if the baby was 'one of those little fellows who had literally to be wrapped in cotton wool and needed everything that medical science knew to coax him to hold on to life.'

The sincerity of this man, who wanted so much to be a father but was destined never to have children of his own, came through in his broadcast and money began pouring in to the hospital. Guy, himself, also received more than 4000 letters in answer to his appeal. He was especially moved by the letters which enclosed money in gratitude for the work being done by the RAF and by those from parents who sent gifts in memory of their sons lost in the air war. He was heartened by the gifts sent by school girls and boys and commented that the air service would never lack recruits.

In the middle of May the first reunion of 617 Squadron was held, marking the first anniversary of the Dams raid. The tables for the dinner had been arranged in a large V shape by putting one table at the base and the rest in two lines at 45 degrees to the base. The resulting empty triangular space where the front of the base table and the ends of the other two lines of tables joined was covered by a tablecloth.

After the dinner was over a large cake was brought in and put on the table at the base of the V. Guy was called upon to speak and stood up on his chair to do so. Being short, he decided it would be better if he stood on the table and climbed up to stand in front of the cake. Unfortunately no one had told him that this part of the table consisted merely of a tablecloth with no support. As his foot hit the gap he fell backwards into the cake, showering those closest to him with pieces of cake and icing. Guy emerged from the ensuing laughter and confusion with the irreverent remark that it had been a long time since he had had a piece of cake between his legs!

Although the reunion had been a time of fun and laughter, it must also have been one of sadness and frustration for Guy: sadness for the loss of his friends who had died that night a year ago and also for the loss of his dog; frustration for while the Squadron continued to operate he was stuck doing PR jobs. This was his Squadron. He had been responsible for its inception. Under his leadership it had grown and flourished. He had overseen the training of the men who had performed the greatest feat so far in the aerial war. For his work with this very special unit he had been given the highest award the country had to offer. Now he sat on the sidelines while someone else was the CO of *his* Squadron. It did not seem fair that only one year after his own moment of glory he should have been reduced to making speeches and begging to be allowed to return to operational flying.

In June, 1944, he was posted to HQ 55 Base at East Kirkby, Lincolnshire, as a staff officer. East Kirkby had become a base station the previous April and was responsible for the airfields at Strubby and Spilsby and for the four squadrons based at these airfields: 280 Squadron at Strubby, 207 at Spilsby and 57 and 630 at East Kirkby itself. The Squadrons all operated Lancasters and East Kirkby took over the maintenance of these aircraft.

Guy's position as a staff officer was non-flying and, once again, he had to submit to the boredom of a desk job. By now he was becoming quite depressed. His life, somehow, seemed to be coming apart and he had not flown seriously for over six months. He found it hard to believe, after the attention he had received the previous year, that he should suddenly have been forgotten again.

147

Unfortunately for him, while he was being fêted in Canada and the USA, life in the RAF had gone on. Other crews were making their mark and he was being left behind. He was not jealous of others as some have said and he did not begrudge them their own moments of glory but he did feel that he was being unnecessarily left out. He believed that he still had a lot to contribute in the air war and he was not being given the chance to make this contribution.

The authorities had a different viewpoint and his pleas to be returned to operational flying fell largely on deaf ears. To them he had become more of a propaganda weapon than a pilot. He had made so many sorties that he was almost unique in the RAF. If he continued to fly and was not so successful in the future the publicity might seriously damage morale, not only within the RAF but among the population as a whole. Guy Gibson was too valuable to lose and, if that meant that he became more and more unhappy in his non-operational role, it was a price that had to be paid.

Perhaps if his personal life had been happier he might have found the inactivity easier to bear but, by now his marriage was all but over. He and Eve still spent some time together and attended public functions whenever necessary, but the magic was gone. Guy had had enough and told Eve that he wanted a divorce. She was upset and still felt that, given time, the marriage could be made to work, but Guy was determined that they should part.

It was in this unhappy state of mind that Guy tried to make the best of his desk-bound job. He hated to be away from the action and was becoming more and more depressed. At the end of June he managed to make a flight, but it was not an operational trip and did nothing to satisfy his longing to return to ops.

In July things began to look up a little. At the beginning of the month he made his first flight in a Lancaster since the previous summer when he went with Squadron

Leader Wyness, 'B' Flight Commander from 57 Squadron, on a short non-operational trip. Better still, on 10 July he received a visit from Micky Martin who had, by now, been promoted Squadron Leader. Although he too was officially in a desk job, he had managed to get himself back on ops. and was flying a Mosquito from Little Snoring, in Norfolk. He took Guy for a flight in his Mosquito which only served to make him more determined to return to flying duties.

With this in mind he drove to London to enlist the help of his cousin Janet's uncle. Sir George Christopher, a ship owner, was Director of Commercial Services at the Ministry of War Transport. He was responsible for organizing convoys and Guy felt that someone in this position might be able to intervene on his behalf. He met Sir George at his office in St Mary Axe in the City of London and drove him, at break-neck speed in his sports car, to his home, Trencrom, in Reigate, Surrey. He was not sure if Sir George would be able to help him, but he was becoming so depressed with his lot that he was willing to try anything. Not surprisingly, this effort was abortive.

On 19 July Guy made his first operational flight since the previous August when he took a Lancaster of 630 Squadron on a daylight raid to the flying bomb site at Creil, north-west of Paris. There was considerable opposition from enemy fighters on the outward flight but the target was reached with no difficulty and was successfully bombed. The return trip was much quieter than the outward and he brought his aircraft safely home after a flight of just over four hours.

This flight, as far as Guy was concerned, had been easy. He could not understand why he was encountering so much opposition to his returning to operational flying and he was determined to do something about it.

Chapter 11

AN EASY TARGET

On 2 August, 1944, Guy was posted once more, this time as a staff officer to No. 54 Base at Coningsby. It was, perhaps, another attempt to keep him out of the air, but was to be no more successful than the last. Guy was determined, at all costs, to return to operational flying.

He had been approaching various influential people in an attempt to get some support for his efforts. When he arrived at Coningsby he found that he had an ally in the base commander, Air Commodore Sharp.

Air Commodore Sharp had been the liaison officer for Bomber Command at the 8th Air Force headquarters of the US Air Force. When he returned to Coningsby he brought with him a P-47 Thunderbolt which, after a few flights, he decided he did not like very much and he exchanged it for a P-38 Lightning. At the beginning of August Coningsby received its second Lightning from the USAAF. This one was, however, slightly different as it was a two-seater with a glass nose and two external tanks situated under the centre section. It was sent to Coningsby for trials.

On 10 and 11 August Guy took this Lightning for two short flights around Lincolnshire and called in at his old base of East Kirkby. By 18 August it appears he was ready to take it on an operational flight and, seemingly with the approval of Air Commodore Sharp, took off on his 74th bombing mission for the airfield at Deelen. On the 21st he made a quick trip to Northern Ireland, possibly to Langford Lodge where Coningsby's other Lightning was to be converted to a two-seater, before making his final op. in the Lightning on 22 August. Shortly afterwards the aircraft was returned to Glatton, from whence it had come.

Although he had made these two trips, they were both unofficial and, therefore, done 'on the quiet'. Guy had no intention of continuing his RAF career in that way. The war was still on and, although things were looking better after the Allied landings of 6 June, there was still plenty to do. When he was in Canada and America Guy had told the crowds to whom he spoke that he fully intended to continue the fight until the Japanese had also been dealt with. Sitting in an office would not accomplish this task.

The more he thought about it the more convinced he became that his entire energy must be directed towards helping to win the war. His private life was in tatters and he needed the challenges that operational flying would give him to help him overcome the situation. At this stage his life was not happy at all. It was not enough for him that he had done more than almost anyone else in the RAF. He was a pilot who flew aeroplanes, not chairs. It was unfair that he should be treated like this but he could not find a way to change things. It seemed that his reward for doing the best he could was to be ignored and kept away from the one thing that he loved best, flying.

He dropped in to the Mess at Woodhall Spa one day. As he walked in no one looked up or acknowledged him. He asked: 'Don't you know who I am?' and was greeted with many rude replies. Some people thought that he was too full of his own importance and that he had come back from the USA and Canada with inflated ideas of himself. While this is not beyond the realms of possibility, these were characteristics that he certainly never showed while on his overseas tour. It was in fact quite the opposite. Everywhere he went in Canada and America people had commented on his modesty and his ability to not take himself too seriously.

It could be that the question 'Don't you know who I am?' was rhetorical. Perhaps he really believed that they

151

did not know. Why should they, when he hardly knew who he was himself any more? Only a year ago he had been at the top; the man of the moment in the air war. now he was nothing. His superiors would not listen to his pleas to be allowed to return to operational flying. His contemporaries dismissed him as being too full of his own importance, living on his previous glory. Less experienced crews, new to the squadrons, did not really know what to think of him. They had been told he was a great pilot; a hero, and yet he did nothing. Even though he was not getting along very well with his wife, it would have been nice to have had her support in his quest for further action. This, too, was denied him. She did not understand his desperate need to be in the thick of the fray and was happy that he had a desk-bound job.

On his 26th birthday on 12 August, Guy met Eve for lunch at a hotel in Skegness. He was tired and very depressed and again told Eve that he wanted a divorce. There did not seem to be any point in prolonging a marriage that was, for him, at least, over. Eve was still not convinced that it could not be saved. She wanted to try and again asked Guy to wait until the war was over before deciding what he was going to do. Wearily he agreed to wait for a few months but told her, in no uncertain terms, that he would not change his mind. He was certain that he wanted a divorce.

The meeting and, therefore, Guy's birthday was not a happy occasion. When lunch was over Eve went back to London to her camouflage netting factory and he returned to Coningsby.

This encounter with Eve had only served to depress him even more. He was sure that the only thing that would drive this feeling away was to be allowed to go back to flying officially. And this, of course, was the one thing that he was not allowed to do.

In this troubled state of mind Guy decided that he could not cope with the idea of a political career. He thought long and hard about withdrawing from the candidature, before finally contacting Mr Weston to tell him of his decision. He then wrote to the Macclesfield Conservative party.

The letter, dated 23 August, began: 'It is with profound regret and only after the most careful consideration, that I have decided to ask your committee to release me from my adoption as the Prospective Conservative Candidate for the Macclesfield Division.' He went on to say how much he regretted any trouble he had caused, but said that the demands of his service career were so exacting that he could not combine them successfully with a political career and do full justice to both. He stressed that he would not be seeking adoption in any other constituency as had been suggested in the press. The committee reluctantly agreed to accept Guy's resignation and sent him their sincere good wishes for his future service career.

His decision to pull out of the political field at this point is, perhaps, slightly puzzling. If everything had gone according to plan he would not have needed to combine a service and a political career. The Conservative party were well aware of his decision to remain in the RAF until after the war and had accepted this condition before electing him as prospective candidate.

It is quite possible that his inability to persuade his superiors to let him return to flying had a bearing on his resignation. As a politician he knew that he would often have to fight hard for the rights of his constituents. It would not be easy and, in his mind, he had already demonstrated his inability to move people with his arguments. He desperately wanted to help the servicemen returning from the war, but he could increasingly see a lack of interest in what they wanted. His own case illustrated that point very clearly. If he was unable to get what he felt he needed, how would he ever be able to do anything for others? He could see that things had not really changed with the war. When it was all over the people who had done most to win a victory would be left behind and the country would, once again, be ruled by the older politicians and industrialists, the very people he had wanted to replace. He had become so discouraged and had lost such a lot of confidence in his own ability that resignation was the only course open to him.

September began as August had ended with Guy making trips in a Mosquito, borrowed from 627 Squadron at Woodhall Spa. They were of no great consequence but they fixed in his mind the idea that his operational flying, when it recommenced, would have to be with Mosquitos. Although he had had very little experience on these elegant wooden aircraft he had flown them enough to be impressed with their performance and knew that he would have to use one for his next operation.

Always a keen photographer, he was given the task of taking a cine film of the Lincolnshire countryside from the air. He made the trip in an Airspeed Oxford and took with him Wing Commander Woodroffe, a controller or 'master bomber' at Coningsby. Three days later the same pair were once again making cine films but this time from a Mosquito on a raid over Le Havre. Two non-operational flights followed in a Lancaster, before Guy was, once more, making films, this time of a Lancaster over the Fens, taken from an Oxford. He had not remained in the RAF for this, but it was better than nothing and certainly more fun than his desk job.

In the middle of September, while visiting the nearby station of Woodhall Spa, he met a WAAF Intelligence Officer whom he remembered from his days with 106 Squadron at Syerston. She was the one he had mistakenly sent up on a flight with a new pilot. They had never been friends as such, but Guy was pleased to see a friendly face from the past and, calling her by her first name, Susan, asked her if she would go for a drive with him around the perimeter track. She thought it a very strange request, and one which she would normally have refused, but something in his manner made her change her mind and she agreed.

Guy just wanted to talk. He needed a sympathetic ear, but although they spoke for quite a while he never opened up to her completely. She did learn, however, that he felt he constantly needed to prove himself both to his superior officers and to the novice crews. All his old confidence and bravado had left him and she could see that he was deeply depressed. Although she tried to help, it was difficult when he disclosed so little of what he was really feeling.

In a desperate attempt to get back to operational flying, he eventually contacted Sir Arthur Harris, head of Bomber Command. He was sympathetic to Guy and eventually agreed, against his better judgement he later said, to allow him to make one more trip. This was hardly what Guy had wanted either. He had already been making the odd trip here and there and one more would not make much difference. However, this one would be with official permission and so could be tackled in a more open way.

It was stressed that the trip must be a relatively easy one and should be as close as possible to Allied lines. The raid on the targets of Rheydt and München Gladbach was the one chosen for Guy and he was to act as master bomber or controller.

His eagerness to prove himself to his senior officers perhaps explains why it was decided to have three different marking points, marked by green, red and yellow target indicators. This was not a method usually employed and would require a lot of careful monitoring and co-ordination by the controller. Certainly Guy had never attempted anything like it before, but if he managed to pull it off it would be impressive. Perhaps then the officers who were keeping him desk-bound would realize that his talents were being wasted and would allow him to return to a Squadron.

The raid was planned for the night of 19 September and

was to finish off what the Squadron had begun the previous week when they had sent out a number of aircraft, along with those of other squadrons, to the same targets on 10 September.

The controller on that occasion had been Wing Commander Charles Owen of 97 Squadron. He briefed Guy on the raid and was dismayed when Guy told him that he intended to ignore the planned homeward route which was to fly south-west over France and instead to take the most direct route home and fly at a very low level. Wing Commander Owen strongly recommended that Guy stick to the planned route, but he could see that his words had fallen on deaf ears.

The day before the raid Guy had a visit from an old friend, John Searby. He arrived from Wyton in a Percival Proctor and had lunch with Guy at Coningsby. They spoke about low-level marking of targets and Guy was enthusiastic as he spoke of the possibilities of this technique. It was evident, however, that he was not happy with his present ground job and was longing to get back to some action.

As Guy had not been operational for such a long time he did not have a regular navigator for this flight. When he went looking for one he found a young Irishman, James Warwick, who had been transferred to 54 Base at the end of August. He was in the process of being posted to 627 Squadron, but this had not been completed. Acting Squadron Leader Warwick had been a Flying Officer at the beginning of the year but had been promoted twice in quick succession, first to acting Flight Lieutenant and then, before this promotion had been confirmed, to acting Squadron Leader. He was 23 years old but, though an excellent navigator, also had very little experience of flying in Mosquitos. Like Guy, he too, was going through an unhappy time in his life having recently received a 'Dear John' letter from his girlfriend.

Rheydt and München Gladbach, close to the Dutch

border were important targets. Both were industrial towns and Rheydt was an important railway centre. It was the meeting place for two major railway lines, one from Aachen and the other from Cologne. Having formed one line at Rheydt this then continued for a mile or so until it reached München Gladbach from where it connected with the main line from the Ruhr into Holland. The railway yards at Rheydt were capable of handling 2500 wagons every 24 hours.

In addition to the communication centre, both towns were actively engaged in heavy industry, making a variety of items including signalling apparatus, electric generators, cables, transformers, motors and oil tank installations. The destruction of these industries would be a major blow to the Germans.

Both towns were, of course, well defended, but had been at the receiving end of heavy bombing only nine days before and had not yet managed to bring their defences back up to full strength.

For the raid that September evening, Guy was allocated the 627 Squadron reserve Mosquito, KB213 AZ-R. This was an aircraft that Guy had flown before but he said he would prefer to take the Mosquito usually flown by the 'A' Flight Commander. This aircraft was KB267 AZ-E. Why he requested this change of aircraft is not known. It could have been that he had had previous difficulties with the reserve Mosquito. The reason may simply have been that KB267 was the newest aircraft on the Squadron. Whatever the reason, Guy was granted his wish and drove over to Woodhall Spa from Coningsby to pick up the aircraft. A big panic then ensued as the ground crews removed the Target Indicators which had already been loaded into KB267 and reloaded them into KB213, which the 'A' Flight commander would now be using.

While all this was going on Guy bumped into his old fitter from 83 Squadron days, the man who had painted the 'Admiral' signs on the Hampdens, Gerry Garton. The two men exchanged a few words, recalling 83 Squadron and also the 617 Squadron first reunion which they had both attended the previous May. Then it was time for Guy to leave and he and Squadron Leader Warwick climbed into their Mosquito and took off for Coningsby from where they would be leaving for the operation.

The raid itself began with rough weather on the outward flight. By the time Guy reached the target, however, this had cleared and the only problem then encountered was some ground haze.

This was to be quite a big effort with over 200 Lancasters dropping a total of 652 tons of bombs on the unfortunate German towns. Nine Mosquitos made up the marking force, in three groups of three, with Guy in the tenth aircraft.

The first target to be marked was the railway junction close to München Gladbach and this was done with the yellow TIs. The town itself was marked with green TIs and here a slight problem occurred when one of the TIs disappeared through a factory window and was only visible from the north. The others marked quite accurately, however, and Guy ordered the main force to bomb only those points which were quite clearly visible in the SE and SW corners of the factory.

Then it was the turn of the town of Rheydt to be marked with red TIs. Unfortunately the first marker had arrived late and the force sent to bomb the red markers was kept hanging around the target while they waited for him to arrive. Although the defences were not too strong, it was less than ideal to have such a large number of aircraft flying round in circles and Guy decided that the red force should bomb the green indicators. Almost as soon as he had made this decision the red markers arrived and accurately placed their TIs. Guy immediately cancelled his previous order and the red force bombed Rheydt.

The damage done to the town of Rheydt was quite extensive and fires were seen right across the town. Just before 22.00 hours a huge explosion was seen and the smoke from this then obscured the target.

München Gladbach had fared even worse. The town was very heavily damaged, mainly by fire. The worst destruction being in the north-east and north-west where the Meere Ag. machinery works was completely gutted. Six other factories were also severely damaged.

In spite of the problems he had encountered Guy seems to have been satisfied with the results and he congratulated everyone over the radio before sending them on their way home.

For the first time in many months Guy had been doing something that stretched his ability. It was what he did best and he felt alive and exhilarated to be over the target directing the raid. As usual he had done a very professional job but now it was time to head for home himself. He set course for England, taking the most direct route as he had told Wing Commander Owens he would, flying north-west over Holland at a low level.

He never reached England.

Chapter 12

THE FALLEN HERO

Steenbergen is a small rural town in the Dutch province of North Brabant. In September, 1944, it was still under German occupation, although it was liberated a few weeks later. The people of the town were used to the sound of aircraft overhead and were always heartened when they saw British aeroplanes. It was the only sign they had that the war was continuing and that eventually the Germans would be defeated and their country would be returned to them once more.

On the night of 19 September, 1944, a local farmer, Mr Van der Riet, had just gone to bed when he heard a terrible crash in the field just beyond his house. Leaping from his bed, he rushed to the window and looked out, but was unable to see much because of a heavy mist which hung over the field. The farmer's two teenage children had also heard the noise but could see no more than their father.

Normally his curiosity would have sent Mr Van der Riet out into the field at once to investigate, but with the Germans still occupying the town this was too dangerous. There was still a curfew in force and so the farmer had to wait until the following morning to discover what it was that had disturbed his sleep. There had been such a noise that he was convinced it was a stray bomb.

The next day dawned and, bright and early, Mr Van der Riet went with his children to the field from where the sound of the crash had come. A horrible sight greeted them and they quickly realized that it had not been a bomb, but an aeroplane crashing, right there on their farm. The aircraft was completely wrecked and there were no signs that anyone would have been able to survive such a crash.

Not wanting his children to see any more, the farmer took them hurriedly back to the house where they waited for some of the men from the town to come to clear up the wreckage. The Germans had banned groups of people gathering together and for this reason the work was left to just three men, Mr Van Mechelen, Mr Stoffelen and Mr Bakx.

At first they thought that there had only been one man in the aeroplane as they only found one body, which had been thrown from the main part of the wreckage and was resting on the ground in front of a small shed. They changed their minds, however, with the upsetting discovery of a third hand.

The local carpenter was sent for and he hastily made a small coffin in which the remains of both men were carefully laid. The coffin was then carried to the mortuary in Blauwstraat, in the centre of the little town.

Although the Allied forces were rapidly advancing into the area, the Germans still had a firm control over the town and, hearing that the local people intended to give the two airmen a proper funeral, the *Ortskommandant* stepped in and ordered that they be buried immediately, without any ceremony.

The people of Steenbergen were, however, determined that there should be a proper funeral. They wanted to do honour to the men who, they believed, had died as much for their freedom as they had for the freedom of Great Britain. Never having been faced with this situation before, they, nonetheless, managed to organize themselves very quickly.

Protestant and Catholic clergymen were alerted and word was sent to the nearby village of Halsteren that they needed to borrow the horse-drawn hearse. This was hurriedly dispatched to Steenbergen and arrived in time for the coffin, draped in the Dutch flag, to be placed on it for the procession to the cemetery.

A group formed behind the coffin, headed by the Dutch deputy mayor, Mr C. Herbers. The mayor, himself, was not present. He was a Dutch Nazi named De Graaf who had fled a few days before the crash, fearful of the advancing Allied troops.

With Mr Herbers walked the town clerk, Mr J. L. M. Jurger and the two clergymen; Pastor J. K. Van den Brink of the Dutch Reform Church and Father Verhoeven, a Roman Catholic priest. The small procession turned out of Blauwstraat and made its way down the town's main street, heading south-east out of Steenbergen. Although they had not been allowed to join in the ceremony, the people of the town watched from their windows and paid their respects to Guy and to Jim Warwick as best they could.

Almost on the south-eastern edge of the little town the procession came to a stop when it reached the ornate double gates of the Roman Catholic cemetery. Turning in through the gates, the coffin was carried along the tree-lined path until half-way down, on the left-hand side, the final resting place of Guy Penrose Gibson and his navigator, James Brown Warwick, was reached.

Since the townspeople did not know the religions of either man, the two clergymen performed the burial service between them; one reading a psalm; the other reciting the Lord's Prayer in English.

Whilst searching through the wreckage in Mr Van der Riet's field the salvage party had found a number of personal items. These included the identification tag belonging to Jim Warwick and an envelope addressed to him. There were other items which appeared also to belong to the Squadron Leader, a signet ring, engraved with the letters JBW and a booket entitled *Instructions and Hints for Fishing*. Some of the other things found could have belonged to either man: a black tie, a damaged

Omega watch, an epaulette from a uniform jacket, a button, a forage cap and some French, Belgian and Dutch banknotes.

From the items found the townspeople were sure that they had the correct identification of one of the men. The only clue to the identity of the other was a sock with a label bearing the name Guy Gibson.

After the Germans left the area a cross was erected to mark the grave of Jim Warwick and Guy. Painted on the top was a Union Jack and underneath were the words '156612 Sqn/Ldr J. B. Warwick, DFC. and Guy Gibson RAF. 19-9-44.'

It was only much later that the people of Steenbergen realized who Guy was and then the cross was amended to show his name and rank at the top, followed by the details of Squadron Leader Warwick.

There has been much speculation since that day in September, 1944, as to the reason for the crash of KB267. It must remain speculation for, although many plausible theories have been put forward, there is no way of knowing the truth.

Perhaps the most puzzling story is that told by the crew of a 61 Squadron Lancaster. They had taken part in the successful raid that Guy had just directed and had heard Guy give them and others a verbal pat on the back and send them on their way home. Minutes later they again heard Guy's voice. This time it was to say that he had lost an engine and was losing height. His final words were, 'I'm trying to make it home.' After this nothing more was heard. Guy did not sound at all distressed; he was just reporting the situation in a matter-of-fact way. The crew of the Lancaster were surprised when they found that he had not returned and even more puzzled when it became clear that no other crews had reported hearing his message.

If the aircraft had lost an engine, for whatever reason, it should have been able to fly perfectly well on the other.

Guy did not give any reason for why he thought the engine had malfunctioned. There is no way of knowing whether they had been hit by flak or whether there was a technical problem.

The possibility of the aircraft having been hit by flak is fairly remote. Although there were defences over the target, the crews from the other squadrons who participated in the raid say that it was so slight that Guy would have had to have been very unlucky for this to happen, although four of the Lancasters sent out on the raid were, in fact, lost.

A more likely solution to the puzzle seems, unfortunately, to lie with the crew themselves. The two men, although both very experienced, had not had the chance to develop into a team. They had not flown together before and were unused to each other. They had not reached the stage in their partnership where a word or gesture was all that was needed from one to tell the other of something that needed to be done.

In a Mosquito the navigator sits lower and slightly to the rear of the pilot on his right-hand side. Behind the pilot's seat are the fuel cocks, used to transfer the fuel between tanks and engines. Since these were in an awkward position for the pilot to operate, this was usually left to the navigator on a given sign from the pilot.

Neither Guy nor Jim Warwick had had very much experience flying Mosquitos. There is the slight chance that neither of them knew the location of these fuel cocks, since they were positioned in a different place from most other aircraft. There is also the possibility that they did know where they were, but that one of them changed them without letting the other know and that the one who had not been told moved them back again, starving the engines of fuel. One eye witness in Steenbergen has said that a light was shining in the cockpit and that the two men could be seen looking downwards as if searching for something. Perhaps this was a frantic effort to rectify the situation when they realized that the fuel transfer had been mismanaged.

This is, of course, pure speculation, but the flames seen streaking from the engines are consistent with the theory of fuel mismanagement. An engine starved of fuel in this way would certainly produce such flames.

Whatever the reason for the crash the loss of one of Bomber Command's best known heroes was a devastating blow to his family and his friends. To have been through so much and to have participated in so many really dangerous missions only to die on what was judged to be a raid on a soft target was a tragic irony.

Sir Arthur Harris, the man who had allowed Guy 'one more flight', was to say, right up until his death in 1984, that he felt he had been wrong to let him go. In truth there was not much that he could have done. Guy had been making sorties off the record before he approached Sir Arthur and would, no doubt, have continued to do so had permission been refused for this trip.

Chapter 13

AFTERMATH

Before setting out for what was to be his last flight, Guy had taken a phone call from Eve. He was rather short with her and told her that he was very busy but that he would call her the next morning. The morning came and went with no phone call.

That afternoon Eve answered a knock at the door and was handed a telegram, marked 'Priority'. Tearing it open she read, 'Regret to inform you Wing Commnder G. P. Gibson (39438) reported missing on operational flight on the night of 19/20th September.' Eve could hardly believe what she was reading. She, like everyone else, thought Guy was indestructible and she was sure it must be a mistake. Guy was much too resourceful to let that happen to him. Later on, when Eve thought more about it, she knew it was true, and she then realized it was what she had been expecting ever since she and Guy were married.

Although his family and close friends knew Guy was missing, nothing was reported in the newspapers. For a time it was thought that there might be a chance that he had baled out and was trying to get back home. Since he was, allegedly, on Hitler's hit list for his part in the Dams raid, his failure to return to England was kept quiet to spare him any problems should he be trying to evade capture in enemy territory. By the end of November all hope for him had been abandoned and reports began to appear in the national press. The *Daily Telegraph* air correspondent, Air Commodore E. L. Howard-Williams MC (Rtd), wrote an article on 30 November in which he put forward a theory that Guy was going to be awarded a posthumous bar to his Victoria Cross. Where the story came from is not known and it did not prove to have any basis in fact.

In December Eve Gibson received a letter from Winston Churchill in which he said:

'I have been awaiting an opportunity to write to you about the loss of your husband. I can assure you that I write in no formal sense.

'I had great admiration for him – the glorious Dambuster. I had hoped that he would come into Parliament and make his way there after the stress of the war was over, but he never spared himself nor would allow others to spare him. We have lost in this officer one of the most splendid of all our fighting men. His name will not be forgotten; it will forever be enshrined in the most wonderful records of our country.

'May I express to you my profound sympathy in the loss you have incurred, and my earnest hope that you will find in yourself those resilient and heroic qualities of which your husband was the proud possessor.'

In an unusual start to a meeting held by the Macclesfield Conservative party, a prayer for the life and safety of Guy Gibson was said. During the meeting Mr Garfield Weston spoke of Guy's magnificent war feats and said how the association of the town with the name of Guy Gibson had done honour to Macclesfield. Speaking of the fact that the new prospective candidate, who had been chosen to replace Guy, was also an RAF officer he concluded:

'Wherever he may be, in this world or beyond, I'm sure nothing would please him better than to know that one of his outstanding officers was to take his place.'

The man that Garfield Weston had described as one of Guy's outstanding officers was, in fact, an Air Commodore. Such had been the impact of Guy's personality on the MP that he had completely failed to notice that the new candidate greatly out-ranked the former.

The first newspaper articles about Guy mentioned only

that he was missing from an operation in September. By January they were reporting his death.

Air Vice-Marshal the Hon. R. A. Cochrane wrote a tribute to Guy which was published in many of the national and regional newspapers. In it he said:

'Wing Commander Gibson had the essential qualities of the operational leader in good measure; his courage was inspiring, his determination outstanding, his clear-sightedness was remarkable for one of his age, his cheerful spirit infectious and his physical fitness for his task unquestionable.

'He stirred up great enthusiasm for physical fitness, a determination among ground staff to achieve the impossible, and among flying personnel to accomplish the exact purpose of the attack.

'He was intensely interested in the tactics to be employed and knowledgeable about the defences in Germany.

'In specific operations he put himself on the order of battle when the opposition was likely to be fierce or the weather so difficult that he did not like having to send his own crews out.

'When he handed over his Squadron to his successor he was beloved by those who did their job to the best of their ability.

'He did not stint his praise; neither did he mince his words of criticism, nor refrain from blunt speaking when neccessary. He had become an inspired leader, full of courage and determination, and it was with the greatest reluctance that he left operations for what appeared at that time, to be for good.

'He was, however, soon recalled for active service and was given the task of training the Squadron which was to destroy the Möhne and Eder dams. He entered upon this task with whole-hearted enthusiasm and quickly organized the necessary training. He studied the problem down to the minutest detail, but it was his own personal leadership which ensured the success of the operation.

'After the award of the Victoria Cross for this operation, and over the whole period of his service in Bomber Command, he set out on a goodwill tour of the United States. He had quite clearly in mind what was required of him. On returning from America he attended the RAF Staff College, from which he came back to his old Group as a staff officer. At about this time he had thoughts of entering politics after the war, but he came to the conclusion that this was not his line of country and decided, instead, that he would make the RAF his career.

'He had already shown that he possessed remarkable grasp of detail and that he could handle staff work well.

'He was, however, most anxious not to drop out entirely from operational work, and it was at his own insistent request that he was finally permitted to act as master bomber on what appeared likely to be a simple operation.

'He completed the control of the operation and was heard telling the force that the attack was completed and that they should return to base.

'From every point of view he was a remarkable man and would have gone far in any walk of life. He will long be remembered in the group in which he served for his infectious enthusiasm, his determination to surmount any and every difficulty, and his sound common sense.'

The Times published, at the beginning of February, a personal tribute from the Warden of St Edward's School in Oxford and there were many other articles written about Guy, extolling his virtues and, inevitably, giving an account of his most famous raid, that on the Ruhr dams.

On 4 February, 1946, 18 months after Guy's death, his book *Enemy Coast Ahead* was published. The previous summer some of the chapters had been serialized in the *Sunday Express* and were very well received. The book itself had excellent reviews. Howard Spring in the *Sunday Graphic* said it was a grand book, full of action from end to end.

The introduction to the book was written by Sir Arthur Harris and was his personal tribute to Guy. His admiration for the young pilot was clear and it was, perhaps, this which clouded his judgement somewhat when he said that Guy was 'not only admired but loved by all who knew him'. He was certainly not loved by everyone, but there can have been very few men who knew him who did not respect his leadership qualities and his courage.

In 1948 Eve Gibson remarried and went to live in South Africa. Her new husband, Jack Hyman, was a South African fruit exporter and for a time Eve was happy with her new life. However, the marriage was not many years old when it began to fail and eventually ended in divorce. Eve returned to England and set about changing her name from Hyman to Gibson once more.

There had been some talk, during the war, of an American film company making a movie about the Dams raid but it came to nothing. Then after the war, a book entitled *The Dam Busters* was published. It was written by Paul Brickhill and detailed not only the Dams raid but the other missions undertaken by 617 Squadron later in the war.

When the head of Associated British Pictures read the book, he decided it would be an excellent story to film and the part of Guy Gibson would be just right for one of the company's young stars, Richard Todd. He purchased the rights to the book and a screenplay was written by R. C. Sherriff.

For two years the film company and Richard Todd researched the subject. The man appointed to direct the film was Michael Anderson. He insisted that it should be filmed in black and white as he wanted it to have the feel of a documentary and could use the original black and white footage that had been taken during the tests for the actual raid. Richard Todd spoke to Eve Gibson and to Alexander Gibson, Guy's father, who each gave their impressions of the man.

The dog picked to play the part of Guy's dog Nigger was an army dog, trained in mine detection. He had never been involved with film work before but behaved beautifully. There was only one strange incident involving the dog. In one scene he had to go past the place where the real Nigger was buried. He could not be persuaded to go near the grave nor could he be dragged past it, but in all other respects he behaved like a veteran actor. In the years since his death many people claim to have seen the ghost of Nigger. Maybe the army dog could see something that was invisible to the other actors?

The film was released in 1954 and, in order to accommodate all the celebrities who had been invited, had its première over two nights. It was a huge success and became a favourite of the wartime Prime Minister, Winston Churchill.

The music, chosen to accompany the film was called appropriately enough, *The Dam Busters' March*. This was composed by Eric Coates and two different recordings of the music reached number 20 in the Hit Parade in October and November, 1955, played by the Central Band of the Royal Air Force and by Billy Cotton's band.

The march itself was not a new composition. It had been written some years before to commemorate the Battle of El Alamein, but had not been published. When Eric Coates was approached and asked to write a march for the new film he took his old composition and re-worked it until he came up with the now famous melody.

In 1955 Air Chief Marshal Sir Francis Fogarty, KCB, KBE, DFC, AFC presented the RAF commemorative window to St Edward's School. This was to be a permanent memorial to the old boys of the school who had been killed whilst serving with the RAF and, of course, included Guy who was the only holder of the Victoria Cross to have been educated there. This memorial was closely followed by the endowment of the Guy Gibson scholarship by the Air Council.

After the war Eve Gibson lent Guy's medals to the Imperial War Museum, where they remained until 1956. That year she decided to assign them to Guy's father for the rest of his life. He was, by then, 79 years old and wore the medals for the first and only time in a Remembrance Day parade that November. He then handed them over to St Edward's School where they remained in the Memorial Library until after his death in 1968, at the age of 91.

In his latter years Alexander Gibson often spoke of his pride in his son, something he had never done while Guy was alive. In May, 1967, he was invited to attend the Air Fair at Biggin Hill. Here he named what was then the last flying Lancaster in Britain *Guy Gibson*. The aircraft had been given by the French Air Force to the Historic Aircraft Preservation Society and was flown to England from the Pacific.

The original plan had been for the aircraft, following the naming ceremony, to carry Dr Barnes Wallis and surviving members of the Dams raid up to Scampton for their 24th reunion. It was also planned that a model of the Dambusters taking off on the raid should be carried in the Lancaster. This model had been made by John Roast, who was the projects director of the Historic Aircraft Preservation Society. In the end Dr Wallis travelled to Lincolnshire by more conventional means on the recommendation of his company, the British Aircraft Corporation.

After the war the Commonwealth War Graves Commission removed the cross marking the graves of Jim Warwick and Guy Gibson and replaced it with two headstones. There had been some talk of bringing the bodies back to England for burial but this was impractical as Guy was English and Jim Warwick came from Northern Ireland so they had no common area that could be regarded as home for their reburial.

The Commonwealth War Graves Commission then suggested that perhaps it would be better if they were moved to the huge war cemetery in nearby Bergen op Zoom. The people of Steenbergen were against the idea as they thought of both Guy and Jim Warwick as their heroes. The matter was settled when both Eve Gibson and her father-in-law said that they thought Guy's body should remain where he had first been laid to rest.

In 1967 a Dutchman named Jan Van den Driesschen discovered that Guy Gibson was buried in Steenbergen. He had always been interested in the Second World War and the RAF in particular and was excited to discover that one of his heroes was buried nearby. He set off one day from his home in Rotterdam to find the grave and to put some flowers on it. When he reached the small cemetery in Steenbergen he walked up and down the pathways looking for the grave but could not find it. Eventually, after retracing his steps, he found it. The headstone was dirty, covered with leaves and moss and the grave itself was overgrown and completely neglected. Mr Van den Driesschen and his wife, Connie, were horrified and made a vow that they would clean up the grave and keep it in good order in the future. Even when times were hard and they were unable to afford flowers for their own home they always made the hour-long journey to Steenbergen to place flowers on the grave. When the weather was very hot and they had planted flowers on the grave, they came three times a week to water them. Later on a local resident, Sebastian Bastiaanse, offered to water the plants for them so that they could cut down their visits from three times to once a week.

The Dutch people believe that Guy Gibson, along with many other Allied airmen, died while fighting for their freedom and they have no intention of forgetting them. The town of Steenbergen has, of course, expanded since that day in September, 1944. Alongside the field where Guy's Mosquito crashed there is now a small industrial area. Three of the streets in this complex have been named as memorials to the airmen and their aircraft; Mosquitostraat, Warwickstraat and, of course, Gibsonstraat.

In 1976, on the anniversary of the crash, a commemorative plaque was unveiled at the entrance to Steenbergen cemetery by Micky Martin, who was by then Air Marshal Sir Harold Martin. The ceremony was attended by Eve Gibson and Ellen Warwick, sister of Jim Warwick. During the service they stood alongside Prince Bernhard of the Netherlands, who had come to pay his respects. Air Chief Marshal Sir Augustus Walker, chairman of the council of the RAF Association, was also in attendance. As Group Captain Gus Walker he had been Guy's station commander when 106 Squadron had moved from Coningsby to Syerston in 1942. During the ceremony the RAF Germany Band played and the Lancaster, from what was then the Historic Aircraft Flight and is now the Battle of Britain Memorial flight, flew overhead.

Fourteen years later, on 7 May, 1990, another memorial to Guy Gibson and Jim Warwick was unveiled in a park in Steenbergen. The granite stone, topped by the twisted propeller of a Lancaster, was unveiled by Group Captain Leonard Cheshire, VC, one of the wartime leaders of 617 Squadron.

While the Dutch were honouring Guy Gibson he was not forgotten by his own people. The first post-war housing estate to be built in the village of Porthleven has a road named after him. In 1953 a road at the RAF Depot at Uxbridge in Middlesex was also named after him. The people of Penarth, South Glamorgan, have included the name of Guy Gibson on their war memorial. Although he never lived in the town he did stay there on many occasions and they felt that he was one of their own, if only by marriage.

After the war, at the Scouts Imperial Headquarters campsite at Tovil, near Maidstone, six crosses were erected as memorials to the Rover Scouts killed during the war. Guy's cross, the only one for a Victoria Cross holder, stood at the centre, taller than the rest.

West Malling in Kent, the airfield that Guy loved so

much, has a Gibson Road. When the airfield was closed recently, for redevelopment the former Officers' Mess was taken over by the local council for use as its own offices. At the instigation of a Kent aviation writer and historian, Robin Brooks, this building has now been named the Gibson Building and has a commemorative plaque at its entrance.

The composer David Farnon has recently written a march which he has called Gibson's March. It is hoped that the Central Band of the Royal Air Force will be including the march in their performances shortly and will also make a recording.

Because of Guy's connections with Porthleven it was decided to erect a memorial to him in the village. The Chairman of the Parish council, Councillor Michael Gale, had for many years had this project in mind and the plans were going well to place the monument in Gibson Way. There were, however, setbacks and the plan was vetoed by Councillor Gale's colleagues. They also refused their permission for it to be placed by the village War Memorial. In disgust, Councillor Gale resigned. When it looked as if the plans would have to be abandoned, a solution was found and the memorial was eventually placed in the village cemetery. It was unveiled on the 45th anniversary of his death by Mrs J. de Gaynesford, Guy's much loved cousin, Janet.

In 1987 Guy's brother, Alick, died. The following year, on 25 October, Eve Gibson also died after a battle against cancer. After her return to England from South Africa she had taken a variety of jobs and finished her working life as assistant housekeeper at Claridge's in London. She did not marry again and, since she had reverted to using the name Gibson, many people were unaware that she had ever remarried after Guy's death. To many people she remained, as she wanted to be, Guy's widow.

Nearly 50 years after the untimely death of Guy Gibson his name has not been forgotten. It does seem that, as

Winston Churchill wrote to Eve Gibson in 1944, his name will for ever be enshrined in the most wonderful records of our country.

He was not a remarkable child. One could never imagine the small, mischievous boy from the broken home being a great leader of men. The teenager of average ability showed none of the qualities which were to mark him, a decade later, as one of the heroes of the Second World War and yet the qualities were there.

He was not especially clever at school yet his determination got him through his exams. His determination to succeed showed again when he refused to accept the RAF's first verdict that he was not suitable officer material because of his short legs. He was ambitious. He could be ruthless in the pursuit of these ambitions and yet his ruthlessness was tinged with a humour that somehow softened it. He worked hard and was completely single-minded in his search for excellence. He also played hard. When he allowed himself time to relax nothing could spoil his fun. In his dealings with others he tried to be fair. He asked nothing of them that he had not first asked of himself and was generous in his praise of a job well done.

He did not suffer fools gladly and was impatient with incompetence or laziness. He could be short-tempered and rude at times and he expected in everyone the same degree of dedication that he himself possessed. He could be intolerant in situations he did not understand and he was not above 'pulling rank' on odd occasions. Where others would try to include all ranks as being equal, Guy did not, unless the other man was known to him personally. He tried to be fair, but he did not always get it right. He was, like us all, an imperfect human being.

Guy's compassionate side was one that was usually well hidden. When it did surface it was all the more unexpected for having been hidden. In situations that would have tried the patience of other men, Guy could have endless patience and understanding. He never minded helping anyone who truly needed help but would not lift a finger for anyone who made a fuss about nothing.

Guy loved anything little and helpless: children, dogs, cats, birds, anyone toward whom he could be protective. He once found a bird with a broken wing and nursed it back to health. When asked why he bothered, he replied that he knew how it felt to be able to fly and he could not bear to think of a little bird who, after all, spent most of its life on the wing, not being able to have that experience again.

Although his career was so successful, he seemed unable to repeat this success in his private life. He longed for a normal family life and yet the one relationship which could have brought him this was a failure. It was certainly not all his fault and, once he had decided that it was over, he did nothing to make it work. He liked women very much but, some say, he regarded them as playthings. To the end of his life he never seemed able to find the woman who could give him the affection he craved and yet allow him to live his own, dangerous lifestyle without complaint.

His propensity for plain speaking did not endear him to everyone, but he did not allow this to worry him at all. He accepted the fact that it was unrealistic to expect everyone to like him, but he was fiercely loyal to those he considered to be friends and that loyalty was returned in full. His own crew would have followed him to the ends of the earth and back, such was their faith and trust in him and his abilities.

It has been said that Guy Gibson was fearless. To believe that is to do the man a great disservice. Courage can only exist where there is fear and courage was something he had in full measure. He had a very real fear of fire, especially in the confines of an aeroplane. Once when he was filling his petrol lighter, some fuel spilled on to his hand. As he went to light his cigarette the fuel

177

on his hand caught alight and, seeing the flames, he fainted. He fought this fear every time he went flying and it was a cruel twist of fate that sent him to his death in a burning aeroplane.

Sir Arthur Harris said that he 'quite wrongly' allowed Guy to return to operations. Perhaps his error was not in allowing him to return, but in delaying his return to operations. Guy loved flying. It was what he lived for and he was not happy doing anything else. Without the operations and without the companionship of his crews Guy was lost. He did not function properly in an office. He completed the tasks in his usual thorough fashion, but his heart was not in his work.

Being grounded was a punishment to him. To many it would have been a welcome reprieve from the horrors of war, but to Guy it was torture. He felt, wrongly, that he had to keep proving himself to his superiors and that his accomplishments so far were not enough. They, in turn, felt that he had done more than enough. Both sides in the argument were wrong, Guy's because he misunderstood the reasons he had been taken off operations; his superior officers' because, in trying to keep him away from operations and, hopefully, save his life, ensured that the last few months that Guy spent on this earth were desperately unhappy.

Like him or loathe him, no one could deny that he deserved better. Everyone deserves happiness in some form or another, especially when they have given so much to ensure the freedom and happiness of others. Death has no respect for heroes and, in the final analysis, Guy was just one of over 55,000 men from Bomber Command who died during the Second World War. In their own way they were all heroes, but Guy Gibson was one of the best.

Appendix I

IMPORTANT DATES IN THE LIFE OF GUY GIBSON

12 August, 1918	Born in Simla in India.
1924	Gibson family return to England.
1926–32	Pupil at St George's Preparatory School Folkestone.
1932–36	Attended St Edward's School, Oxford.
1935	Oxford & Cambridge School Certificate.
1936, Nov.	Joined RAF.
1937, Feb.	Posted to No. 6 Flying Training School, Netheravon.
1937, Sept.	Posted to No. 83 Squadron, Turnhouse.
1938, Mar.	83 Squadron moved to Scampton.
1939, Jun.	Promoted to Flying Officer.
1939, Sept.	First operation of the war to bomb Kiel on day war broke out.
1939, Dec.	Met Eve Moore in Coventry.
1939, Dec.	Death of mother.
1940, Feb.	83 Squadron detached to Lossiemouth.
1940, Jul.	Dropped Bomber Command's first 200lb SAP bomb on the city of Kiel.
1940, Jul.	Award of Distinguished Flying Cross.
1940, Aug.	Shot down Do215.
1940, Sept.	Posted to No. 14 OTU, Cottesmore.
1940, Sept.	Promoted to Flight Lieutenant.
1940, Oct.	Posted to No. 16 OTU, Upper Heyford.
1940, Nov.	Posted to 29 Squadron, Digby.
1940, Nov.	Marriage to Eve Moore.
1941, Apr.	29 Squadron moved to West Malling.
1941, Jun.	Promoted to Squadron Leader.
1941, Sept.	Awarded Bar to DFC.

1941, Dec.	Posted to 51 OTU, Cranfield as Chief Flying Instructor.
1942, Mar.	Posted to HQ 51 Group
1942, Apr.	Promoted to Acting Wing Commander.
1942, Apr.	Posted to 106 Squadron as squadron commander.
1942, Nov.	Awarded Distinguished Service Order.
1942, Nov.	Dropped first 8000lb bomb on Italy.
1943, Mar.	Last operation with 106 Squadron.
1943, Mar.	617 Squadron formed.
1943, Mar.	Posted to 617 Squadron as squadron commander.
1943, Mar.	Awarded Bar to DSO.
1943, May.	Raid on Ruhr Dams.
1943, May.	Awarded Victoria Cross.
1943, Aug.	Left for Canada and USA as part of Prime Minister's party for Operation Quadrant.
1943, Oct.	Awarded Legion of Merit by General Arnold in Washington, D.C.
1944, Jan.	Posted to Directorate of Accidents at Air Ministry.
1944, Jan.	Began writing *Enemy Coast Ahead*.
1944, Feb.	Appeared on BBC programme, *Desert Island Discs*.
1944, Mar.	Elected Prospective Conservative candidate for Macclesfield.
1944, Jun.	Posted to HQ 55 Base, East Kirkby, as staff officer.
1944, Aug.	Posted to HQ 54 Base, Coningsby, as staff officer.
1944, Sept.	Last operation as Master Bomber on raid to bomb Rheydt and München Gladbach.
1944, Sept.	Killed on night of 19 September and buried in Dutch town of Steenbergen on 20 September, 1944.

Appendix II

AIRCRAFT FLOWN ON OPERATIONS BY GUY GIBSON 1939–1944

83 SQUADRON.

Handley-Page Hampdens

L4057: *Admiral Imaz Dryazel*
L4070: *Admiral Foo Bang.*

29 SQUADRON.

Bristol Blenheims

L1303
L1327
L1502

Bristol Beaufighters

R2094
R2140
R2138
R2144
R2146
R2148
R2150
R2182
R2183
R2196
R2246 in which he scored his first victory.
R2250 in which he scored the rest of his victories.

R7627
R7622
R7641
R7673
L6712

106 SQUADRON.

Avro Manchesters

L7319
L7485
L7418
R5770
L7378

Avro Lancasters

R5845
R5673
R5678
R5637
R5899 – 'F'
R5901 – 'U'
R5750 – 'Z'
R5779 – 'C7'
R5637 – 'D'
R5551 – 'V'
R5611 – 'W'
W4118 – 'Y' *Admiral Prune*
W4127 – 'G2'
LM303 – 'M'

617 SQUADRON.

Avro Lancaster III

ED932 – AJ-G.

55 BASE.

Lockheed P-38 Lightning

LOB26

54 BASE.

de Havilland Mosquito

KB213
KB267

Appendix III

CITATIONS FOR AWARDS

Distinguished Flying Cross awarded 9 July, 1940.

'For gallantry and devotion to duty during air operations.'

Bar to the Distinguished Flying Cross awarded 16 September, 1941.

'This officer continues to show the utmost courage and devotion to duty. Since joining his present unit, Squadron Leader Gibson has destroyed three and damaged a fourth enemy aircraft. His skill was notably demonstrated when, one night in July of 1941, he intercepted and destroyed a Heinkel 111.'

Distinguished Service Order awarded 20 November, 1942.

'Since being awarded a bar to his DFC this officer has completed many sorties including leading a daylight raid on Danzig and an attack on Gdynia. In the recent attack on Le Creusot, Wing Commander Gibson bombed and machine-gunned the transformer station nearby from five hundred feet. On October 22nd, 1942 he participated in the attack on Genoa and two days later he led his squadron in a daylight sortie against Milan. On both occasions Wing Commander Gibson flew with great distinction. He is a most skilful and courageous leader whose keeness has set a most inspiring example.'

Bar to Distinguished Service Order awarded 2 April, 1943.

'This officer has an outstanding operational record, having completed one hundred and seventy-two sorties. He has always displayed the greatest keenness and in the past two months has taken part in six attacks against well defended targets, including Berlin.

'In March 1943 he captained an aircraft detailed to attack Stuttgart. On the outward flight engine trouble developed but he flew on to his objective and bombed it from a low level. This is typical of his outstanding determination to make every sortie a success.

'By his skilful leadership and contempt for danger he has set an example which has inspired the squadron he commands.'

Victoria Cross awarded 28 May, 1943.

'This officer served as a night bomber pilot at the beginning of the war and quickly established a reputation as an outstanding operational pilot. In addition to taking the fullest possible share in all normal operations, he made single-handed attacks during his 'rest' nights on such highly defended objectives as the German battleship *Tirpitz*, then completing in Wilhelmshaven.

'When his tour of operational duty was concluded, he asked for a further operational posting and went to a night-fighter unit instead of being posted for instructional duties. In the course of his second operational tour, he destroyed at least three enemy bombers and contributed much to the raising and development of new night-fighter formations.

'After a short period in a training unit, he again volunteered for operational duties and returned to night bombers. Both as an operational pilot and as leader of his squadron, he achieved outstandingly successful results and his personal courage knew no bounds. Berlin, Cologne, Danzig, Gdynia, Genoa, Le Creusot, Milan, Nuremberg and Stuttgart were among the targets he attacked by day and by night.

'On the conclusion of his third operational tour, Wing Commander Gibson pressed strongly to be allowed to remain on operations and he was selected to command a squadron then forming for special tasks. Under his inspiring leadership, this squadron has now executed one of the most devastating attacks of the war – the breaching of the Möhne and Eder dams.

'The task was fraught with danger and difficulty. Wing Commander Gibson personally made the initial attack on the Möhne dam. Descending to within a few feet of the water and taking the full brunt of the anti-aircraft defences, he launched his projectiles with great accuracy. Afterwards he circled very low for thirty minutes, drawing the enemy fire on himself in order to leave as free a run as possible to the following aircraft which were attacking the dam in turn.

'Wing Commander Gibson then led the remainder of his force to the Eder dam where, with complete disregard for his own safety, he repeated his tactics and once more drew on himself the enemy fire so that the attack could be successfully developed.

'Wing Commander Gibson has completed over 170 sorties, involving more than 600 hours operational flying. Throughout his operational career, prolonged exceptionally at his own request, he has shown leadership, determination and valour of the highest order.'

Appendix IV

RESULTS OF THE RAID ON THE DAMS.
16–17 May, 1943

Damage caused to Ruhr valley by breaching of Möhne Dam.

Factories destroyed	11
Factories damaged	114
Bridges destroyed	25
Bridges damaged	21
Power stations destroyed/damaged	9
Water pumping stations affected	15
Houses/Farms destroyed	92
Houses/Farms badly damaged	1003
German dead	476
German missing	69
Foreign dead	593
Foreign missing	156
Cattle and pigs dead	6316

The foreign dead and missing were the inmates of a labour camp situated at Neheim, where the River Möhne joins the River Ruhr. They included 439 Ukrainian women as well as French and Belgian prisoners of war and Dutch male labourers.

The water was 30 feet deep and fast flowing. Many kilometres of roads were washed away and 4000 hectares of farmland were rendered useless.

Damage caused to Eder Valley by breaching of Eder dam.

Workplaces destroyed/damaged	101
Bridges destroyed	14

Power stations out of action	4
Houses destroyed/damaged	112
German dead	47
Cattle and pigs dead	very many

The military airfield at Fritzlar and a large proportion of the industrial area of Kassel were flooded and severely damaged

Several thousand hectares of arable land were rendered useless.

All details are from official German figures and are taken from Operation Chastise, 617 Squadron RAF, 16–17 May, 1943, by Alan Thompson. (Published by Alan Thompson 1992.)

INDEX

George VI, HM King, 30, 115, 116, 121

Gerrards Cross, 137, 144

Gibson, Alexander Edward Charles, 'Alick', 10, 12, 13, 14, 15, 16, 17, 18, 19, 20, 22, 24, 25, 30, 31, 32, 39, 40, 41, 44, 48, 52, 59, 175

Gibson, Alexander James, 5–12, 15, 17, 19, 23, 24, 47, 170, 172, 173

Gibson, Charles, 5

Gibson, Evelyn Mary, nee Moore, 44–45, 49, 52–54, 56, 59–60, 67–69, 71–73, 76, 79–80, 84–85, 89, 113–115, 121–122, 124, 134, 139–142, 145, 148, 152, 166–167, 170, 172, 174–175

Gibson, G. P. Wing Commander
aircraft flown, 181–183
appears on *Desert Island Discs*, 141, 142
arrival of Nigger, 72
award of VC, 144, 115
birth, 10
childhood, 11–13
citations for awards, 184–186
conclusions, 176–178
considers political career, 138–141
crash in Magister, 103
Dams raid, 108–111
death, 3, 160, 161
death of mother, 46
death of Nigger, 107–108
flying training, 29–30
formation of 617 Squadron, 98
funeral, 161–162
important dates, 179–180
investiture at Buckingham Palace, 121–122
master bomber on last flight, 157–159
meets Barnes Wallis, 100
meets Eve Moore, 44
memorials, 172, 174–175
permission for last raid, 155
public relations work, 117–120
publication of *Enemy Coast Ahead*, 169
schooldays, 14, 18–22, 25–28
selection by Conservative party, 143

takes command of 106 Squadron, 76
tour of North America, 125–136
tributes, 166–169
trip with Richard Dimbleby, 90–93
unhappiness at grounding, 152–155
visit to Chequers, 124
wedding, 59
withdraws from politics, 153
writes *Enemy Coast Ahead*, 138

Gibson, Leonora Mary, nee Strike, 6, 7, 8, 9, 10, 11, 12, 13, 14, 15, 16, 17, 22, 24, 25, 26, 45–46, 47, 48

Gibson, Michael Penrose, 59

Gibson, Ruth, nee Harris, 39, 59

Gilze-Rijen, 2

Glasgow, 49, 71, 136

Glatton, 151

Gneisenau, 86

Goebbels, Paul Josef, 92

Göring, Hermann, 92

Golders Green Cemetery, 46

Goss, S. Surgeon-Captain RN., 114

Graf Zeppelin, 86

Graham-Little, Pilot Officer, 64

Grange, The, East Malling, 68, 69

Grange, The, Wellingnore, 58, 60, 62, 64

Grantham, 100, 105, 112

Greenbridge, 134

Gregory, W. J. 'Sticks' Wing Commander, 73

Grieg, Sir Louis Group Captain, 81

Grout, A. Pilot Officer, 71

Grumman Goose, 133

Hain Steamship Company, 6

Hale, Sonny, 44

Halifax, Nova Scotia, 126, 127, 134

Hall, Henry, 21

Halsteren, 161

Hamble, 34

Hamburg, 51, 52, 78, 131

Hamilton, Lady, 145

Hamilton, Lord 145

Handley Page Hampden, 34, 35, 37, 38, 42, 48, 50, 51, 54, 86, 157

Hannah, J. Sergeant, 56

Harris, Sir Arthur T. MRAF, 3, 76, 114, 155, 165, 170, 178